Men Without Friends

DAVID W. SMITH

THOMAS NELSON PUBLISHERS
Nashville

For Sue Ann Smith
who has been my wife
and closest of friends
for the past twenty-seven years

Copyright © 1990 by David W. Smith

Published in Nashville, Tennessee, by Thomas Nelson, Inc., and distributed in Canada by Lawson Falle, Ltd., Cambridge, Ontario.

Unless otherwise noted, Scripture quotations are from the NEW KING JAMES VERSION of the Bible. Copyright © 1979, 1980, 1982, Thomas Nelson, Inc., Publishers.

Scripture quotations noted KJV are from the King James Version of the Bible.

Scripture quotations noted NIV are from The Holy Bible: New International Version. Copyright © 1978 by the New York International Bible Society. Used by permission of Zondervan Bible Publishers.

Scripture quotations noted RSV are from the Revised Standard Version of the Bible, Copyright © 1946, 1952, 1971, 1973. Used by permission.

Scripture quotations noted TEV are from the *Good News Bible*—Old Testament: Copyright © American Bible Society 1976. New Testament: Copyright © American Bible Society 1966, 1971, 1976. Used by permission.

Scripture quotations noted TLB are from *The Living Bible* (Wheaton, Illinois: Tyndale House Publishers, 1971) and are used by permission.

Library of Congress Cataloging-in-Publication Date

Smith, David W., 1943–
    Men without Friends / David W. Smith.
       p.   cm.
    Includes bibliographical references.
    ISBN 0-8407-3128-0
    1. Friendship. 2. Men—Psychology. I. Title.
BJ1533.F8S6 1990
177'.6—dc20   90–33031
                         CIP

1 2 3 4 5 6 7 8 9 10 - 97 96 95 94 93 92 91 90

CONTENTS

_5/_

FOREWORD

The American male is lonely and friendless, but he tries to maintain his macho image at all costs, even if it means isolation from people. The author of this book is concerned for this man. With a warm, personal, and vulnerable attitude, David Smith presents the situation in the reasoned, documented manner of a social scientist, yet with illustrations and insights that give light and guidance.

Dr. Smith is writing from his own personal experience and from information gleaned from four hundred interviews.

Some books for men have an ego-centristic approach, teaching men how to look out for themselves and how to win in the cannibalistic world of business. David Smith, instead, points to the biblical models of men in deep, caring relationships with each other and with women.

Smith's book is not macho, effeminate, or anti-woman. He sees that men need to grow in their ability to have deep friendships in order to become whole persons. Women, as well as men, will gain a more complete understanding of male needs, fears, and insecurities, along with their abilities for relationships. An especially strong and practical chapter is "The Stages of Friendship" where the reader is coached in developing close, lasting, personal friendships.

As you read, you will be convinced that it's okay to be male and to experience warm, caring friendships. It's not just okay, it's necessary!

Jim Conway
Author, *Men in Mid-Life Crisis*
and *Your Marriage Can Survive
Mid-Life Crisis*

ACKNOWLEDGMENTS

I want to express my gratitude to friends who have shared with me from their hearts about friendship and friendlessness. I thank them for their openness and candor. And I want also to express my appreciation to the hundreds of strangers who took the time to be interviewed and to complete a questionnaire for this book. I have learned much from these individuals.

Finally, I want to acknowledge my indebtedness to my wife and closest of friends, Sue Ann Smith. Without her support and patience, this book might not have reached a successful conclusion. Surely without her willingness to listen, discuss, and comment on an endless list of issues related to the book during the last three years, I know the book's final form would have been of lesser quality.

CHAPTER ONE

Who Needs Friends?

Chuck had been perhaps the most hard working salesman in his company's history—at least in recent memory. He usually spent sixty-five to seventy-five hours a week at the office when he wasn't traveling. And when he was on the road, his weekly work hours could run as high as ninety. Of course, no one complained about his schedule. If anything, others were jealous of his success. He generated incredible revenues, beating all the other sales representatives hands down year after year. And his lifestyle showed off his success. His suits were the top-of-the-line, he bought a new car every two years, and his house was worth half a million, not to mention the value of the ten acres of prime real estate on which his house sat. He was even married to one of the most beautiful women in town, and he had two children, both of whom were doing well in school. Of course, he made sure that his family had every material desire they wanted. What more did he (or they) need?

Friends. *Male friends.* He spent so much time working and winning in the marketplace that he had no time to spend developing friendships with other men. Certainly he knew many people at work, and he came in contact daily with clients who relied on him and his expertise. But no one knew Chuck—no one really knew him deep inside. In fact, Chuck had even lost touch

9

with himself. He was so busy achieving and conquering that he came to believe he was what he did. Performance was his identity. If he wasn't selling a client, he was developing sales pitches and ad ideas that would win future clients. Nothing else really mattered to Chuck. This was all he lived for.

Then Chuck retired. He walked out of the office after receiving one of the grandest retirement parties his company had ever thrown. He had worked hard for more than forty years. Now he looked forward to enjoying all the wealth and prestige he had acquired over the years. But he ended up enjoying it alone. Frustrated and hurt from years of neglect, his lovely wife left him. And his children, who had since become adults and left home to begin their own lives, rarely visited him. They really didn't know him, and he didn't know them well either. He had never had the time to spend with them while they were growing up. Now they didn't have the time or the inclination to spend with him. The few times they managed to get together, conversation waned after only an hour, so soon visits were largely conducted on the telephone—about once every two or three months, and then the calls lasted only about fifteen minutes.

Lonely, Chuck tried to keep up a few relationships he had had with some of his former coworkers. They would get together to talk shop, but soon they had little time for him since they were busy meeting the demands of their jobs, just as he had done during his working years.

Within a year after his retirement, Chuck became a stranger—or was he in some sense always a stranger?—at the company for which he had spent his life diligently working. Feeling unwanted and unneeded, he stopped coming around. Calls from his kids also grew more infrequent. Chuck was alone—friendless.

* * *

Jerry was a man's man. He hunted, fished, did all of the maintenance and most of the repair work on his own car, and helped out at his church, occasionally taking care of some of the groundwork. On the job, he was as reliable and self-sufficient as any of the other construction workers. He dated once in a while and at least once a week went out with some of his working buddies for some beer and bowling. Most everyone liked him, and those that didn't at least respected him.

But when Jerry was diagnosed with cancer, his buddies became strangely quiet and uncomfortable. And when he went into the hospital for chemotherapy treatments, except for occasional visits from his pastor, no one came to see him. And even his pastor spent no more than half an hour every few days with him.

A year later, when Jerry died, some of his buddies carried his casket, one of his old girlfriends came and cried a bit, and his pastor delivered the eulogy, but no one really knew Jerry. So his funeral was brief, and the tears shed were few. Jerry died alone—friendless.

Everyone depended on Frank. When anyone had a problem, Frank took the call. Sick and in the hospital? Frank would be the one who would make the visit. Need a projector for a Sunday school class? Frank would make sure it was there and in working order. Marital problems? Frank was the best at solving them. Hassles with a boss at work? Frank's counsel was always helpful. Kids out of control? Frank could help parents decide what to do. Frank was "Mr. Fix-it." No matter the problem, no matter the time of day, Frank could be expected to respond with a sensitive smile, a warm embrace, and sound advice.

But whom could Frank talk to? To whom could he turn when *he* had a problem? As the church's minister, Frank knew that people were fragile and that everyone needed a friend—someone they could depend on, share their deepest struggles with, and completely open up to. Frank had tried to find such a person, but soon gave up. Whenever he shared a confidence, it swept through the church in a matter of days. And some of the men on his own church board refused his attempts to build friendships with them, arguing that he needed to learn to depend solely on God for his relational and spiritual needs.

So Frank withdrew, not from his work, but from vulnerable contact with people. Sure, he poured out his needs and desires to God, but his need for human companionship—his hunger for male friends—went unmet. For four years he lived this way, struggling to meet the needs of his parish while perishing on the inside. Then, he turned in his resignation, left his parish, and entered the life insurance business.

As a minister, he had been alone—friendless. Perhaps as an insurance agent, he could make some friends. At least he wanted to try.

Although Chuck, Jerry, and Frank found themselves alone, they were not alone in our American culture. Most American men suffer the same friendless condition that they did. Interestingly enough, however, many of them don't even know or care that they have no friends.

This book is for men and for those who know men who need friends. I have written it to help men see their need for friends and to show them how they can enrich their lives by making and maintaining friendships with other men. Many women don't need the counsel given in this book for their own lives because they actively seek friendships, nurture them, and benefit from them. Men, on the other hand, usually don't try to make friends and don't know how to keep a friendship once they have one, so they rarely benefit from whatever friendships they have. What men have with other men is generally a coworker or buddy relationship, not a friendship.

What Is *Friendship?*

Aristotle defined *friendship* as "a single soul dwelling in two bodies." Ralph Waldo Emerson said a friend is a person with whom one can be sincere.

I asked my wife, Sue Ann, for her definition of friendship. She thought for a moment and then simply responded "Lois." Friendship to Sue Ann, as to most of us, is a personal experience that exemplifies far more than a one-sentence definition.

One of the finest examples of male friendship is found in the historical record of 1 Samuel in 18:1–3, 23:15–16, and 19:1–7. Here we read about real male friendship, about a relationship that ran deep between Jonathan, the king's son, and David, a shepherd boy and God's future choice for the throne. Their friendship was strong, built solidly on an inward attachment rather than on an outer attraction or social status. The King James translation of the Bible says "their souls were joined together." These men demonstrated a mutual acceptance of each other despite their different social backgrounds. Covenant or promise rather than performance permeated their friendship. Jonathan did not have to do favors for David, and David, for example, was not pressured into killing more giants such as Goliath to remain Jonathan's friend. Their promise to be faithful to each other was born of unconditional love (18:3). Consequently, they stood strong together and refused to rely solely on self (23:15–16). Mutuality, not individualism or competition, marked their friendship. Moreover, they were not selfish but loyal to each other (19:1–7). David's interests were more important to Jonathan than his own, and David felt the same way about Jonathan's interests.

If you study the friendship between David and Jonathan, you will walk away with a good understanding of what a healthy friendship between men can and should be like. Concluding from their relationship, I would say that any definition of friendship should include the following:

- Unconditional love
- Personal enjoyment
- Mutual acceptance
- Mutual interests
- Mutual commitment
- Mutual loyalty

In short, friendship involves a concern for and involvement with the well-being of another.

Friendship Made Personal

But where are *you* in regard to friendships? Do you have any friends? If so, what is the quality of your relationships with your male friends? One way to answer these questions is through some self-analysis. Take a few minutes to examine your own male friendships by answering the following questions. They are not designed to embarrass you or to compare you to someone else. Rather, they are here to help you assess what could and should be a very important and enriching aspect of your life—your friendships with other men. So take a risk. Answer the questions—honestly.

1. Do you have any friends—men who allow you to be vulnerable and authentic, and who support and encourage you regardless of your social status, occupation, or situation?

2. Are you a friend to other men?

3. Are you afraid to show emotions, such as fear or sadness, in front of other men?

4. Do you believe that you must always be in control of yourself and your situation?

5. Do you take time to write or call other men for no other reason than to find out how they are doing or to share with them something personal about yourself?

6. When you make a promise to another man, do you keep it?

7. Do you pray regularly for your friends?

8. Do you remember your friends' birthdays, anniversaries, or other special occasions with a phone call, card, or other form of acknowledgment?

9. Do your friends count on you to keep a confidence?

10. Do you reach out and help your friends without expecting any kind of repayment?

11. Do you seek advice from your friends?

12. Do you accept criticism from your friends?

13. Do your friends feel close enough to you to offer advice or to come to you for advice?

14. Are you truly yourself when you're with other men?

15. Do you hold grudges?

16. Do you respect your friends' opinions and beliefs, even if you disagree with them?

17. Do you listen for the emotion coming through your friends' words?

18. Do you stay in regular contact with friends who are separated from you by many miles?

19. If you have a falling out with a friend, do you take the initiative to mend the relationship?

20. Are your friends' social status and material possessions important foundation blocks for your relationship with them?

If you answered "Yes" to questions 1, 2, 5–14, and 16–19, and "No" to questions 3, 4, 15, and 20, you are probably in good shape as far as your friendships with other men are concerned. If any of your answers varied from these, you probably have some areas in your life that need attention if you are ever to develop satisfying friendships with other men. Regardless of your answers, however, you can benefit from the content of this book if you approach it openly and seek to apply its counsel. I'm not saying I have perfect friendships. I'm a fellow struggler. But I do know from my own experience, the experience of others, and my own research that what follows works.

Focusing on Friendship

Below I have listed seven ideas about friendship which form the central focus of my discussion in this book.

1. Friendships in which we give and receive are essential to our spiritual and emotional well-being.
2. Most American men are actually friendless and have much to learn in the development of interpersonal relationships.
3. Men, including spiritually oriented men, lead lives that conform largely to our macho-dominated culture rather than to the standard found in the Bible.
4. Women tend to experience more fulfilling friendships than do men, and the reasons for this difference are not biological.
5. Biblical principles of friendship can be identified and, if implemented, change lives. The Bible offers the best psychology of friendships available.
6. Those who have close, nurturing friendships have

many personality traits in common that can be learned.

7. With the decline in the social stability of the extended family and the nuclear family itself, friendships are becoming even more important than ever before for the maintenance and maturity of mental and spiritual health.

Throughout this book, we will examine the validity of these seven statements and see how they apply to men in general and each of us men in particular. We will also answer other questions that have further practical import for all men—such questions as: How many friends do people usually have? Do women have more friendships than men? Why are women more successful with friendships than men? Why are friendships with the opposite sex so rare? How do friendships develop? What are the basic personality traits of a good friend? What principles of friendship are offered in the Bible? How does age, marital status, or religion affect friendships? What can women do to help men form more satisfying friendships? What can men do to help themselves in this area of their lives?

Much is known about the many relationships we experience as adults. Writers have provided the public with abundant information dealing with marriage, family, sexuality, in-laws, workaholism, and countless other topics. And yet little knowledge and few publications exist which provide us with an understanding of the dynamics of male friendships. Most everyone has opinions and prejudices on this subject, but few people have conducted actual research.

In preparing to write this book, I recalled my own ideas and personal experiences about male friendship,

FRIENDSHIP RESEARCH SURVEY

I am conducting research dealing with the topic of friendship and American men. Thank you for taking the time to express your opinions about the issues listed below.

David W. Smith, Ph.D.

Questions for Men and Women

Define the term *close friend*.

How many close friends do you have who fit your description in the first question?_____ Same sex_____ Opposite sex_____

Are you satisfied with the quality and quantity of your friendships? Explain.

What can you do to improve interpersonal relationships with others?

Do you and your close friends share similar beliefs and interests (for example, in religion, politics, values, or hobbies)?

What are your obligations or responsibilities in a friendship?

I would welcome any other general comments you would like to share on this topic. And thank you for your involvement with this research.

and I read what others have written about friendship. I also spoke with dozens of my friends and acquaintances about this neglected topic. Although this approach would normally provide sufficient research before starting to write, I decided to go one step further and prepare a questionnaire. I talked with complete strangers in both Indianapolis and Chicago shopping centers and asked these individuals to respond to my brief survey. In all I talked with approximately 750 people, 430 of whom were willing to spend a few minutes to give their personal response to my questionnaire.

Even though I interviewed personal friends, neighbors, members of my church, and some of my colleagues at work, almost all of my questionnaires were completed by total strangers. Strangers were often more open, I found. They had no image or reputation to protect since they didn't know me and they realized they would probably never see me again.

I talked with both men and women, young and old, rich and poor, married and divorced, well-educated and not so well-educated, religious and non-religious. Individuals passing by were asked if they would mind taking a few minutes to give their answers on the questionnaire dealing with friendship shown on the opposite page.

Much of what I learned from the data gleaned from this survey is reported in this book. I don't claim that my efforts at data collection were scientific, but I enjoyed the process and found the results extremely valuable.

In addition to these questions, I asked respondents for personal background information, which included their sex, age, marital status, income, occupation, education, and religion. The information they shared with me is listed in percentages on the next page:

SURVEY RESULTS OF PERSONAL BACKGROUND

Sex		Age		Marital Status	
Males	47%	18–25	17%	Married	41%
Females	53%	26–35	18%	Single	20%
		36–45	24%	Divorced	21%
		46–55	17%	Remarried	7%
		56–65	12%	Spouse deceased	11%
		66 and older	12%		

Income		Education	
Under $15,000	25%	High school or less	27%
$15,000–25,000	29%	Some college	20%
$25,000–35,000	22%	College graduate	35%
$35,000–45,000	18%	Graduate school	18%
$45,000–55,000	4%		
Over $55,000	2%		

Religion		Occupation	
Protestant	65%	Professional	29%
Catholic	24%	White collar	18%
Other or none	11%	Blue collar	24%
		Other (homemaker, student, unemployed)	29%

A Personal Note

I have written this book, not so much as a social scientist, but as a man who has experienced the hurts and frustrations of unrealized or unfulfilled friendships. I have also known the joy and satisfaction that comes from a close friendship. More of what and who I am as a man is revealed in these pages than I originally intended. I, like most American men, am reticent about revealing much of my true self, but writing a book about male friendship required that I be authentic and open.

I want to share with you from my experiences and the

experiences of others. I have tried to avoid offering a simple, hackneyed, or dogmatic formula for improving relationships. In fact, this book represents only one stage of
my personal search for better relationships with others.
I'm an impatient person, too preoccupied. My busy life
still gets in the way of my giving to and receiving from
friendships. I am not in any way a perfect example of how
best to be a friend. What I am is simply a fellow pilgrim
searching for and trying to contribute to relationships
which are rich and satisfying.

You and I were designed to enjoy healthy relationships
with other men. We don't have to be lonely or go through
life with a John Wayne mentality of macho independence.
So join with me to discover the world of friendships we
were meant to enjoy.

CHAPTER TWO

The Best Property of All

We take care of our health, we lay up money, we make our roof tight, and our clothing sufficient, but who provides wisely that he shall not be wanting in the best property of all—friends?
—Ralph Waldo Emerson

A prosperous East Coast businessman seemed to the public to have it all. Ron was sophisticated and urbane. To his neighbors, acquaintances, and fellow workers he appeared well read, well dressed, and well prepared for any situation. His intelligence, successful career, and home and family in the suburbs presented the image of a man who lacked nothing.

But the private Ron was quite different from the public image. Every night and during most of each weekend, he drank, read, and watched TV. His wife found it sadly ironic that this man who was so proud of his extensive vocabulary was usually silent and noncommunicative at home. Her concern turned to anger and finally to indifference after years of living with a man who was either unwilling or unable to reveal his emotions. To both his wife and teenage children, Ron was merely a stranger who prompted feelings of frustration more often than love.

His drinking and failure to communicate finally led to separation and divorce. Ron now lives alone. Not yet fifty years old, he has had one heart attack. He no longer drinks, but his health has not improved. With professional help he is trying to learn how to express his feelings better. Unfortunately, his emotional expressions now seem exaggerated. He tends to overreact when expressing his feelings where he used to be expressionless, so that he gets either unduly excited or overly melancholy. His future does not look very good. His friendlessness cost him all he held dear. Now he has no one to share his joys and hurts. He traded the shared life for the isolated life.

Ron's story is the story of far too many American men. In the process of keeping to themselves, keeping people at arm's length, keeping relationships superficial, they sacrifice a lifetime of intimacy, vulnerability, shared burdens and joys. Their skewed picture of independence gives them a relationally empty life.

Men are different from women, for which we all give thanks. Unfortunately, some of the differences between the sexes are far from positive. One serious difference is the way in which men perceive friendships; their entire way of thinking about friends is often unlike that of their female counterparts. In his book *The Hazards of Being Male: The Myth of Masculine Privilege*, Herb Goldberg asked adult men if they had any close friends and found that many seemed surprised by the question. "No, why? Should I?" was the usual response. Goldberg wonders if men perceive their isolation, their lack of friendship with other men, as normal.

Some distinctly male characteristics are of course natural and good (see Chapter 5), while others tend to be harmful. These first chapters explore why many men live in a way that hinders or even prevents the making and keeping of close friendships with other men.

What are some of the barriers to true friendship between men?

Aversion to Showing Emotions

Very early in life little boys receive the cultural message that they are not supposed to show emotions. *Expressing feelings is generally taboo for males.* From an early age boys hear the words "Don't be a sissy"; "Big boys don't cry"; "Aren't you a little too old to be sitting on your father's lap?" The message comes through loud and clear—boys must learn to be men, and men must conceal their emotions.

In the mid-seventies America witnessed on network television the return of many war-ravaged prisoners from Vietnam. Some of these POWs had not been seen by family or friends for a decade. Many relatives had feared the worst—that the one they loved and missed so much might even be dead. Therefore, the long-hoped-for reunions were packed with emotion. Yet mothers often reacted differently from fathers as they saw their sons for the first time in years. Mothers and wives were open with their expressions of emotion, but with few exceptions fathers were reserved. I watched one father on TV simply extend his hand to the son he had not seen in years.

Except for acts of violence or in contact sports, such as football, men do little touching of one another. Touching implies sexual interest to many men. The thought of hugging someone as an expression of affection or friendship without sexual overtones is hard to accept. Some men become irritated or, more likely, embarrassed if they are hugged by a friend. Perhaps men shun physical expressions of feelings with men because of the unconscious fear of latent homosexual tendencies. Boys learn early in life that males are not supposed to touch each other. Fathers hug their daughters, but at best only rough and tumble with sons. Mock fighting is common between fathers and sons.

This aversion to showing feelings of affection is a very common barrier to finding or becoming a friend. In fact, it can even distort a man's understanding of friendship.

Inability to Fellowship

Men find it hard to accept that they need the fellowship of other men. The simple request, "Let's have lunch together," is likely to be followed with the response, "Sure, what's up?" The exchange makes it clear: the independent man doesn't need the company of another man. The image of the independent man is that he has few if any emotional needs. Therefore, men manufacture nonemotional reasons for being together—a business deal must be discussed or a game must be played. Men often use drinking as an excuse to gather together. Rarely do men plan a meeting together simply because they have a need to enjoy each other's company.

Even when the same men are frequently together, their social interaction may remain at a superficial level. Just how long can conversations about politics and sports be nourishing to the human spirit? The same male employees can have lunch together for years and still limit their conversation to sports, politics, dirty jokes, and the sexual attractiveness of selected female workers in their office or plant. They do not know how to move their conversation to a deeper level for real fellowship.

Inadequate Role Models

As we enter the 1990s, we are still beset with Rambo-style models for manhood. Our TV and movie heroes help to perpetuate the male problem of friendlessness. Heroes tend to be self-sufficient, strong, and impersonal. They usually avoid long-range emotional entanglements. Personalities such as those portrayed by James Cagney, John Wayne, Sean Connery, Sylvester Stallone, Tom Selleck, and Arnold Schwarzenegger are examples of hard, independent men who use rather than love both women and men. They neglect or ignore children. Even in the 1990s men who spend too much time with kids are believed to be effeminate.

The major emotions these role models provide are anger and bravery. In the classic film *High Noon*, Gary Cooper epitomized American masculinity in a supreme display of bravery. When he was challenged, the woman he loved implored him to avoid the fight, but he felt he had no choice. While all others turned away in cowardice, Cooper stood alone against a gang of thugs. This image of manliness is quite rigid and difficult to live up to in real life.

Our media heroes are usually violent. While many television programmers have recently turned more to displays of cheap sex to attract viewers, they continue to develop so-called action shows which reveal our interest in violent acts. Television programming both leads and reflects public opinion. Certain shows like "The Equalizer" illustrate the public's fascination and respect for violence. How does the hero solve problems? He gets angry and becomes violent. One learns that problems can be solved quickly (the average show is sixty minutes in length) by physical action. Patience, compromise, and long-suffering are seldom traits of masculine characters.

These models of toughness have led many men to respond to real or imagined challenges to their manliness in ways that are actually dangerous. They are quick to respond to a dare, or what seems to be an insult to their pride. Who participates in barroom brawls? Who tries to cut off another motorist on the road? Who engages in shouting matches or trades insults? Of course, women are capable of physical violence, but usually men turn to violence to settle a dispute. Men tend to believe that the *real man* has a natural capacity for violence.

Sadly, the mask of aggressiveness and strength tends to keep us men from knowing ourselves or each other. Fears, joys, loves, hopes, and concerns are largely kept within, preventing us from forming close friendships.

Inordinately Competitive

Men feel they have to excel at what they do in life. If a man plays a game, he feels he must win. When Jimmy Carter was President, he played baseball with the press corps. The competition was intense. President Carter really wanted his team to win. Carter also concerned himself daily with White House tennis action. He wanted to know who had played whom and the outcome of each match. Winning was very important to him.

John Kennedy's sister, Eunice Shriver, described how her brother hated to lose at anything. In fact, "The only thing Jack ever got emotional about was losing."

No doubt about it. Winning is more important to us than how we play or even how we live.

Parents often compare the personal achievements of their sons with the accomplishments of other boys. A boy learns that other boys are his competitors and, therefore, potential enemies. This kind of thinking is reinforced with time and works to undermine the development of close relationships between men.

Competition is very highly respected among men. Vince Lombardi, the great Green Bay Packers football coach, used to say, "Winning isn't everything; it's the only thing." Many coaches as well as corporate executives have held to the belief that nice guys finish last. Bobby Knight, the basketball coach at the University of Indiana, has been criticized for motivating his teams with fear, swearing, yelling, and generally undisciplined behavior. Many come to his defense with the simple statement, "But he wins and that's what is important." The end justifies the means. If you can win, all else is forgiven.

Men generally find it difficult simply to have fun. It's hard for them to set aside the burden of needing to win. I must confess that I find it difficult to enjoy a game of tennis unless I win. If I lose I can actually become angry—not at my competition necessarily, but rather with my poor performance. Perhaps I judge my self-worth by whether or not I win.

Of course, there's nothing wrong with friendly competition, but men are so uptight about beating the competition that they often miss out on the joy of participation and the simple fun of being with friends. If men are not good at a sport or an activity, they avoid it. Why do we have to win at what we do? So what if we are not the greatest athlete, singer, trombone player, or whatever?

This notion about the priority of winning extends to mental areas as well as physical. Most men rarely admit to ignorance about a topic. To do so might leave the impression that they cannot compete or are less than all-knowing. During my first year as a teacher, I labored under the false belief that, as a teacher and as a man, I should have all the answers to students' questions. Luckily for me and my students, I soon realized there was nothing wrong with saying, "I don't know." This freed me from the burden of trying to be a walking encyclopedia. The students and I could learn some things together.

Kids won't let you play the all-knowing game. They'll press you for more answers or even say, "Who are you kidding?" Adults, on the other hand, simply keep a know-it-all at arm's length—and therefore friendless and lonely.

When my family was living in a suburb of Chicago, we had a neighbor who tried to convey the impression that he knew virtually everything, regardless of the topic. He became especially forceful in expounding his religious and political opinions at neighborhood parties. We were expected to sit quietly at his feet and acquire wisdom. If we disagreed with him, he became rather emotional or even verbally hostile, as I quickly found out when I challenged his chauvinistic ideas. His all-knowing attitude made him intolerant of the ideas of others.

This man may be a caricature of the average adult male, but most men, like him to some extent, want to be in command of whatever they are doing, be it sports or a conversation. This inordinately competitive spirit is a barrier to friendship.

Inability to Ask for Help

Men will rarely ask for help. It's tough for a man to admit deep personal needs or longings. We seem to be reluctant to seek help for anything from an ailing marriage to an ailing body. Men are reluctant to share problems not only with counselors but even with their own wives or families—and God forbid that they seek help from a friend!

If asked why he refuses to share, a man usually responds that he doesn't want to burden the family (or friend) with problems. He is then that much harder to reach, more removed and aloof.

This resistance to admitting dependency on others is not limited to the major areas of our lives. A woman once attempted to give road directions to her brother-in-law during a trip to a family reunion. He refused to listen and proceeded to drive in the wrong direction for at least half an hour. The woman was furious. "If you don't want to

listen to me," she said, "at least stop at a gas station for
directions." Finally, he did, but by stopping at a filling
station, this otherwise normal male was admitting that he
needed help. The women in the car expected to hear, "I'm
sorry, I made a mistake." However, that was too much for
the man to say, so the carload of relatives drove off toward
their family reunion—in silence.

Boys learn early to stand on their own two feet. "Don't
count on others" or "God helps those who help themselves" are frequent comments of fatherly advice. Boys
who cling too much to parents are potential sources of
embarrassment. When my father was five or six years old,
his father took him to the end of a pier and threw him into
Lake Michigan and said, "Swim." Later he added, "You
must learn to take care of yourself." What my father
learned was not to trust his dad and perhaps all men in
general.

Too much self-sufficiency robs a man of the fulfillment
of his need for the support, love, and concern of friends.

Incorrect Priorities

Men often have a distorted order of priorities. Physical
things are more important than relationships. Status is
obtained by the acquisition of material wealth rather
than, say, the number of close friends. An acquaintance of
mine years ago used to show disrespect for his wife's comments and attitudes by saying, "That's immaterial." It
seems so strange that love, concern, and relationships
should take second place to the material emphasis of so
many men.

This distortion of emphasis on the material is certainly
not a recent development. The Old Testament prophet
Haggai, for example, warned that we are more concerned
about living in paneled houses *(material)* than we are

about our relationship with God and our fellow man *(im-material).*[1]

A man's success is measured by how much wealth and power can be acquired. Divorced men will speak with little shame about their failures at home, but in sharp contrast are quite defensive if they fail in the business world. At a businessmen's lunch a man said, "I have spent the last thirty years reaching the top rung of the world's ladder of success. I now feel in my heart I was for all those years on the wrong ladder." Life had passed him by. Sure he had money, but his wealth was acquired at the expense of intimacy with his family and friends.

Unfortunately, this problem of friendlessness exists even in our churches. In church we sit together and sing together, and we greet one another cheerily as we leave at the end of a service. We do all these things, sometimes for years, without forming any real personal Christian relationships. The church, therefore, becomes a place where Christians live alone together.

I know a man who is dying of a rare disease. His name appears in the church bulletin under the heading "Remember in Prayer." The deaconesses send him flowers, and periodically someone, usually the pastor, will offer a public prayer on his behalf. But to my knowledge, few if any men in the church have gone to spend time with him, to listen and to share—in short, to be his friend. The Bible teaches us that, as we have opportunity, we are to do good unto all men (Gal. 6:10); however, we insulate ourselves from the healthy and the sick alike.

Men simply fear getting involved with others beyond a superficial level. This lack of intimacy is foreign to the biblical command to "bear one another's burdens, and so fulfill the law of Christ" (Gal. 6:2). There is no way to do this while keeping others at arm's length. The Galatian letter (3:27–29) reminds us that we are to enjoy fellowship together, a oneness as believers in Christ. The barriers that separate us should be destroyed.

But the barriers that separate men remain and may even be becoming more formidable. Men pay a heavy price for their unwillingness or inability to remove the barriers which separate them and prevent the formation of friendships. Too many of us still tend to believe the creed of the *real man:*

> He shall not cry.
> He shall not display weakness.
> He shall not need affection or gentleness or warmth.
> He shall comfort but not desire comforting.
> He shall be needed but not need.
> He shall touch but not be touched.
> He shall be steel not flesh.
> He shall be inviolate in his manhood.
> He shall stand alone.[2]

This definition of masculinity or manliness is one of the most significant and distorted within Western culture. A masculinity that is detached, unemotional, and uninvolved is not masculinity at all. We who have consciously or unconsciously assimilated the false masculinity described in this chapter have had to pay a heavy price to live by it. The emotional and physical consequences we have paid are discussed in the next chapter.

DISCUSSION QUESTIONS

1. What are some reasons discussed in this chapter that hinder men from reaching out to other men in friendship and fellowship? Do any of these reasons apply to you personally?

2. How important is winning to you? Discuss the positive and negative characteristics of a lifestyle based on competition.

3. How do you measure self-worth or the worth of another? What role do wealth, influence, and physical strength have in how you define the value of yourself and others?

4. From what source or from whom did you acquire your standard of masculinity? Why do you think it is a standard worth living by? What benefits, if any, has it brought you? What have been its negatives?

CHAPTER THREE

The High Cost of Being Male

We have met the enemy and he is us.
—Walt Kelly in *Pogo*

Modern men are as conditioned mentally as the caveman to slug it out alone with a saber-toothed tiger, but are often unprepared to meet the constraints of living in contemporary modern society. We are an anachronism. We learn early in life to be combative or at least competitive, yet few of us learn to be conciliatory. Few of us value close interpersonal relationships and fewer still seem willing to invest the time and emotional energy necessary for the development of closeness. The fragmentation of community life, corporate pressures, the breakdown of the extended and even the nuclear family, the drive for success, and the rate of mobility have all taken a tremendous toll on the intimate friendships we can acquire and sustain.

How has all this affected our quality of life?

By the traditional retirement age of sixty-five, there are only seventy-five men alive for every one hundred women. It may be an exaggeration to conclude

34

that men are slowly killing themselves, but the grim facts are nevertheless quite frightening. Women, on the average, live a full 7 years longer than men. Life-span projections for baby girls born in the early 1990s have now reached 80 years. For baby boys the projection is about 73 years.

If the forecast of an earlier grave is not bad enough, there is more bad news. The fortunate men who do remain alive into old age tend to have more physical problems than women. In the book *The Total Man*, Dan Benson reports that in marriages where both are elderly and one of the pair is an invalid—it is usually the husband. The onetime strong, independent, competitive man must be cared for by a healthy wife. Benson believes that men who are unable to express emotions or to seek help in time of need or to show gentleness and caring, finally, after many years, pay for it physically.[1]

The way we think and act reduces not only the quantity of life but also its quality. This is a staggering proposition which certainly needs our attention.

Stress: Positive or Negative?

During the 1930s, Dr. Hans Selye first discovered the terrible effects that stress has upon the human body. His work with hormones and the endocrine glands revealed a strong correlation between the way the mind and body function. If you are friendless, lonely, working under great pressures, frustrated, or in other ways maladjusted mentally over a long period of time, you create wear and tear on your body as well as your mind. Psychosomatic disorders—those diseases or ailments that have their origin in your mind—are physically real and can have a devastating impact upon both the quality and the length of your life.

As dangerous as stress can be, we need not fear the frequent pressure-packed moments of everyday living that so often create stress. Stressful experiences are a normal part of a person's social and work life. The available research suggests that it is not so much the amount of stress one experiences that affects mental and physical health but rather the manner in which one handles the stress. If your boss is difficult to work for, this is sure to produce anxiety and stress, but it doesn't have to affect your health or feelings of self-worth.

Many researchers argue that the key to harmlessly venting daily stress is a strong network of friends and family. Breaking ties, as in divorce for example, or never establishing such relationships appears to increase the incidence of heart disease, strokes, hypertension, migraine and tension headaches, rashes, ulcers, and even infectious diseases such as tuberculosis. If we are to avoid their potentially ruinous impact, we must share the frustration, stresses, loneliness, and anxieties of everyday life with people we love and who love us in return.

Physicians Meyer Friedman and Ray H. Rosenman in their book *Type A Behavior and Your Heart* list numerous behavioral characteristics that appear in high-risk heart patients. They include:

- a sense of time urgency
- a persistent desire for recognition and advancement
- a strong competitive drive
- an emphasis on work at the expense of social and family life
- a tendency to take on excessive responsibilities because of the feeling that "only I can do it."

Take notice that these damaging traits are usually associated with men rather than women. Read over the list again. These traits are almost synonymous with what we have learned to believe is male behavior. Women experience stress too, often in larger doses than men. However, even the "Super Moms" who must balance work and home responsibilities seem to adapt to stress and other problems better than most men. *It is how we respond to stress rather than the stress itself that gives us our problems.*

A study conducted by the University of California at Berkeley has shown that American men are among those who have the highest heart disease rates in the entire world. Japanese men, for example, have a much lower rate of coronary disease. Such variables as diet, smoking, and drinking were not as important as lifestyle. Japan is a highly industrialized society with a dense population living within a relatively small archipelago. There are approximately 125 million Japanese living in an area the size of California. Tension and stress from high expectations are present, but emphasis is placed on the importance of family and friends. Because of their priorities, they are able to defuse some of the stresses inherent in many industrialized jobs.

It has been my privilege to meet and act as host to several Japanese teachers and administrators who were visiting the United States. I was impressed with their orientation toward family and friends. Americans tend to think in an "I" or "me" context while Japanese seem to support a "we" mindset. The Japanese seem more likely to view themselves as part of a group than as autonomous individuals. They are responsible to others and want to be in harmony with them. In contrast, Americans strive for freedom and independence.

In the longevity game it is the men with balanced lives who win. They mix work with fun. People who live long, happy lives are not one-dimensional. University of Wisconsin expert on aging Dr. Roger J. Stamp says that these people have learned to pace their lives. "They were responsive and appreciative of the world around them. They liked simple things like flowers, dogs, and northern lights, and they were able to enjoy the traffic along a detour instead of cussing the highway department."[2]

Ronald Reagan is an example of one who has led a balanced life. George Will says that Reagan "has proven that the presidency is not such a destroyer after all. His immediate predecessor, Jimmy Carter proudly, even ostentatiously, made the presidency seem crushing."[3]

Job: Blessing or Barrier

Jack Houston, careers editor for the *Chicago Tribune*, argues that too often a job puts American men in a position of having to choose between their jobs and their friends, spouse, or family. This statement is largely spurious. If a man is forced to choose, then his job is demanding more time and energy than should be either expected or provided. Men can't blame their jobs for their lack of close friendships or close family ties. I think that jobs which are extremely demanding and consume most of a man's energy and time are rare. And men who do work in these positions usually do so of their own free will.

A fifty-five-year-old head mechanic for a large cement company works approximately eighty hours a week. His job and his life are inseparable. He has allowed the job to become not only his principal interest but his only real concern in life. His wife and children rarely see him. He rarely visits his mother or siblings, even though they live in the same suburban area. He doesn't need the money the extra hours produce. His boss would be just as happy if the man worked a normal forty hours. The man's life consists of working, and in the few remaining hours, sitting in front of the television. Subconsciously he avoids the possibility of intimacy at every turn. He uses his job as a barrier to insulate himself from others. His obsession with work ruined his first marriage and has sapped the vitality from his second. He has no real friends and his own children have walked out of his life following years of neglect and rejection.

Dr. John M. Rhoads of Duke University concludes from research that those who give an inordinate amount of attention to their jobs have few outside interests, have little sense of humor, rarely take vacations, and worry about problems when it is inappropriate to do so. While the Bible warns us about the sin of laziness, it also warns us about work that is unnecessarily demanding: "It is in vain that you rise up early and go late to rest, eating the bread of anxious toil; for he gives to his beloved sleep" (Ps. 127:2 RSV).

Our culture teaches us that our performance in the work place leads to money, status, and even power. Richard Huber, in his book *The American Idea of Success*, says that success is not gained from being a loyal friend or a good husband. Rather it is a reward for performance on the job. Acquiring and enjoying material wealth is a pursuit worthy of our attention and is justified in such varied sources as the Bible and Adam Smith, author of early capitalist theory. My point here is not to challenge our desire to acquire wealth. My concern rather is with a *preoccupation* with this aspect of life.

At work, if we're busy or in some way unavailable, we feel this translates into being important and responsible. Yet it is the man who allows himself to become overworked who tends to be the least effective. He's hampered by incidentals. He finds it difficult to say no to virtually any request and therefore may not perform well at any task. If you feel you're not a workaholic but that the company is simply demanding more of your time than is justified, it may be time to look for another job. The book *What Color Is Your Parachute?* by Richard N. Bolles will get you started looking for new employment.

If your job truly prevents you from leading a balanced life, you'll need to make a change if possible. Some superachievers are asking to move to a slower business track at work where they can continue to work hard but without sacrificing a personal life.[4] If, in your judgment, you are too old to change jobs or are locked into a pension plan, perhaps you can change departments or responsibilities without leaving your present employer. Don't cling to a rotten job just because it seems secure.

The Real Problem

For most of us, the real problem is not with our jobs but rather with ourselves. It is not our jobs that create the calamity of our friendlessness and our psychosomatic disorders, but rather how we view ourselves and how we think and behave that get us into trouble. We have learned to withstand and keep to ourselves any pain, loneliness, fear, or other emotion that has a taint of humanness. Indeed, we believe that we have to deny our feelings and have been so taught.

If we fail to reach the required level of insensitivity and strength—the plight of most of us mortals—that failure is likely to produce additional frustrations and the sense of being somehow less a man. Someone once wrote that the birthright of every American male is a chronic sense of personal inadequacy. The problem is not with our failure to reach the standard but rather with the standard itself.

Dan Benson believes that "the American masculine dream is killing us."[5] This unobtainable dream or standard is the Spanish *machismo* concept of a man's being an unswerving pinnacle of strength. He is the nonemotional creature who surmounts all tasks and problems with unfaltering success.

If we repress our emotions, do they disappear? Hardly. Denial and repression force our emotions to be revealed in some distorted fashion either mentally or physically. No man who has been born does not have a basic need for emotional release. We're unable to survive without it. James Wagenvoord believes that:

> A man is never able to completely suppress his inner self. He can hide it, or rationalize it, or diminish its importance, but he isn't able to banish that self permanently. Of course, the continual struggle between what he wants and what he thinks is required of him makes his emotions erupt in fits and starts. A brief explosion of inexplicable tears, an outburst of sudden affection, a late-night confidence—these are the humanizing cracks in his mask.[6]

Men seem to falter in their relationships with others partially because they mentally live in a world that no longer exists. For hundreds of years, and in most cultures, human needs were largely material. The main concern was to survive. Acquiring the basic material necessities of life was a full-time job. Men had little time to do anything but work hard. This emphasis upon survival, however, was altered for most men living in the Western world following the widespread effects of the industrial revolution in the mid-eighteenth century. With advances in farming and science, the average working man, regardless of his social class, has to spend fewer hours acquiring the essentials for biological survival.

But technology changes faster than human attitudes and behavior. People may resist change or, without much thought, follow old outmoded patterns of behavior. Many resist positive change with the exhortation, "But we've never done it that way before."

Despite the removal of the threat of hunger or starvation in Western nations, many among our species still concentrate all of their energies acquiring material wealth as if somehow their very physical survival depends on it. Too much attention is devoted to physical needs at the expense of what might be referred to as psycho/spiritual needs. Just as survival needs must be satisfied, so must our psycho/spiritual needs. If neglected or denied, as is the case with most American men, we will see distorted personalities in varying degrees.

Abraham H. Maslow, the psychologist who greatly advanced our understanding of human motivation, argued that once basic physical needs are met we are then free to concern ourselves with deeper, more advanced levels of human needs. Maslow contended that the physiological needs of food, water, and air are of obvious and utmost importance. Once these are satisfied we are motivated to free ourselves from physical threat or dangers, to obtain a secure physical environment.

But even with a safe and secure physical and material world well assured, many men continue to work as if the wolf were still at the door. The "how-to-succeed" books rarely emphasize that the same qualities which take you to the top can also drop you to the bottom. Personality traits don't exist in a vacuum. A virtue in one situation or time period may well be a detriment in another. Holding in high esteem the values of power, materialism, and status may have served men better in years gone by than today. Achieving bodily comforts and positions of power and prestige does not in itself satisfy, over the long haul, the longings of the human spirit.

The famous Menninger Foundation has provided a do-it-yourself mental health checkup for men to evaluate if serious problems exist in their lives. Ask yourself the same checkup questions:

1. What are my goals in life and how realistic are they?
2. Is my use of time and energy helping me to reach these goals?
3. Do I have a proper sense of responsibility or do I try to do too much and fail to acknowledge my limitations?
4. How do I react to disappointments and losses?
5. How am I coping with stress and anxiety?
6. What is the consistency and quality of my personal relationships? Are my contacts with others superficial, meager, and unrewarding?
7. From whom do I receive and to whom do I give emotional support? Do I avoid getting support from others for fear of appearing weak?
8. What is the role of love in my life? How much time do I give to listen to and care for others?[7]

As you answer each question, you should be able to provide a response that is constructive and that you feel comfortable with. The only important grade on this checkup is that you feel good about your answer to each of the eight questions. Pay particular attention to questions 6, 7, and 8. Answers to these questions alone should give you some idea about the quality of interpersonal relationships you have with others. Most men do not score very well, especially on the last three questions. Our interpersonal relationships tend to be anemic. If we are honest about our condition, if we admit to ourselves that our relationships with others are not what they should be, then we can begin to make corrections.

To free ourselves from the disruptive social and psychological constraints which we have learned, we must first clearly understand our fundamental God-given basic needs. We will turn our attention to this issue in the next chapter.

DISCUSSION QUESTIONS

1. Why is a strong network of family and friendships essential to both the quality and quantity of life?
2. How have we as men valued self-reliance to a distorted extreme? How can you change this situation in your life?
3. Do you agree that aspects of your behavior and attitudes may actually affect the length of your life? What are the implications of this for you?
4. Take the do-it-yourself Menninger mental health checkup. Discuss the test and your responses with another person. What can you start changing in your life to increase your mental health?

CHAPTER FOUR

Basic Survival Needs

The lyric in a song Barbra Streisand sings concludes that "people who need people are the luckiest people in the world." Actually people who need people are the only people in the world. Not everyone is willing to admit it, but each of us needs intimacy with and the nurture of at least a couple of significant other people. Even to ourselves we don't often acknowledge the depth or pervasiveness of our need for human intimacy.

We are more similar than we are different. We focus on our differences but it is our human similarities that unite us. Everything I need, you need too. To define what it means to be human is to list the basic emotional needs we have in common within the human family.

There are six basic needs that are common to all humans in all periods of history and across all cultures, age levels, and social classes. They are universal. If these needs are not satisfied, we can suffer from social dysfunction, mental illness, and psychosomatically induced illnesses.

Just what are our basic emotional soul needs? Psychologists, sociologists, and theologians have studied this question for decades. In the early part of this century, sociologist William Thomas worked on this question, as have Louis Raths, Anna Burrell, and other more recent scientists. Their findings are similar: all **45** humans have six specific major emotional needs that must be satisfied if they are to function as well-adjusted, happy individuals. The person who has these six core needs fulfilled is at peace within and is a contributing member of the society. To reach this state of mind a person must possess the following in ample supply.

Belonging and Love

Each of us needs to be an important part of a whole. We all suffer from an enormous fear of being rejected. The need for belonging is the need to feel worthwhile. Having the knowledge that we are accepted and even loved by others provides us with emotional security. Whether we admit it or not, we also need to belong to and be accepted by God. The ultimate fulfillment of belonging is knowing that we are created by a personal God who loves us. We have worth and dignity not because of what we can do or produce but because we are created beings of Almighty God.

Several decades ago a study was conducted within a South American orphanage. Normal physical care was provided for the babies, but because the orphanage was so badly understaffed, the overworked nurses were unable to play with or show affection to the children. The babies responded at first by crying. Later they lost their appetites, became restless and nervous. More than ninety babies became ill or died solely due to a lack of love. Approximately twenty children survived but were hopelessly mentally ill as they grew older.

In January 1978, a memorial service was conducted in the U.S. Capitol Rotunda for Hubert Humphrey. Washington's elite gathered to say good-bye to the former senator and vice-president. Richard Nixon was there that day, off by himself, as if he were quarantined. Howard Baker, remembering that day, said, "Nobody would talk to him. Everybody was afraid of him." The awkward ostracization of the former president ended only when President Jimmy Carter walked over to Mr. Nixon, shook his hand, and welcomed him back to Washington. *Newsweek* magazine concluded that this simple act of humanity and compassion changed Nixon's future. "If there was a turning point in Nixon's long ordeal in the wilderness, that was it."[1]

Benjamin and Ruth Lippsett met in the 1920s and were married for sixty-two years. They both died last year in Santa Fe, New Mexico, within an hour of each other. The cause of each death was recorded as heart failure. Benjamin was eighty-nine and Ruth was eighty-six on the day they died. Their daughter Betty Ann Rose gave testimony to their wonderful life together. "He adored her from the first time he laid eyes on her, right up to the last time he laid eyes on her. It's listed as heart failure, but that is not what they died from. He stayed until he knew she was gone and didn't need him anymore. That's the way they wanted it. We told Dad Mom had gone. He saw her; then he lay down, cried some tears, and within the hour he stopped breathing."

Army chaplain and theologian Paul Tillich may not have had marriages like that of the Lippsetts in mind when he wrote that "there is no life where there is no otherness," but his words came to mind when I heard their story.

In two independent studies, one a nine-year study at the University of California at Berkeley and the other at the University of Michigan, social scientists found that adults who don't belong to nurturing groups or relationships have a death rate twice as high as those with frequent caring human contact. Dr. James S. House of the University of Michigan, commenting on the Michigan study, says, "The data indicates that social isolation is as significant to mortality rates as smoking, high blood pressure, high cholesterol, obesity, and lack of physical exercise."[2]

People cut off from spouses and friends run a great risk of developing health problems and dying prematurely. We need to belong. Being lonely is hazardous to our health.

While I was in college my grandmother-in-law broke her hip and was hospitalized for several weeks. On the days my wife or I visited with her, the nurses reported that she was alert and happy for the entire day. But if no one visited her in a twenty-four-hour period, she quickly developed a confused and disoriented personality. It wasn't a lack of human interaction that affected her so dramatically since many employees entered her room briefly with food and medication. What was missing on those few days we were unable to visit Grandmother Cameron Malmborg was the awareness of being with family members who deeply loved her.

I agree with Daniel Callahan when he writes in his book *Setting Limits* that the place of the elderly in a good society is an inherently communal, not an individual, question. None of us can function without others. We need the love and affection of other people throughout life.

Accomplishment

Goals, both short-term and long-term, are important to our mental health. People who feel they are not accomplishing all they should in life usually think of themselves as failures. Men need to work toward the successful conclusion of projects large and small.

One of the secrets of longevity is to continue to plan and anticipate. A common trait of those who live in good health to a ripe old age is the ability to live for tomorrow. In Maslow's theory the accomplishment need is referred to as "self-actualization," or the ongoing need to improve.

Each of us has a need to create, to express ourselves, to use our talents, even if no one acknowledges our efforts. I overheard a story about an old Eskimo who lived in the Alaskan wilderness with only goats, ducks, and chickens for company. When he wasn't either searching for or growing food, he spent his time creating beautiful oil paintings of the majestic scenery that surrounded him. These paintings hung on his cabin wall. He did not need an audience. There was satisfaction simply in the creation.

In 1989 the San Francisco area suffered an earthquake that left behind widespread destruction. The majestic Golden Gate Bridge, however, escaped damage. It didn't even buckle. So the day after the earthquake it was reopened for traffic. Dr. Charles A. Ellis, an obscure Purdue University professor, was responsible for the engineering design of this bridge. When it was built during the 1930s and 1940s, Dr. Ellis received little notice for his remarkable engineering contribution. Instead, another engineer, Joseph Strauss, received the public's acclaim because he was more visible as a promoter and fund raiser of the building project. For his efforts, a statue of Strauss sits at the foot of the bridge, but no such monument was erected in Dr. Ellis's honor. Ellis was never troubled by the absence of attention. He believed that self and public acclamation was unimportant. "What really matters," he said, "are the accomplishments we leave behind to the benefit of others."

This is true, at least to some degree. I believe, however, if we have an opportunity to share the results of our creative talents with loved ones or friends, we experience a far deeper satisfaction. Have you ever received a trophy for an athletic or public service accomplishment? Did you store it out of sight of family and friends? My guess is that you displayed it and enjoyed telling others close to you about your accomplishment. Trophies, like any expression of our talents, are for sharing with people who care about us.

Meaning and Purpose

We must have the sense of accomplishment, but we are fulfilling a need beyond what accomplishment alone can provide. Harold Kushner in his book *When All You've Ever Wanted Isn't Enough* says that our lives go on every day.[3] They may be successful or unsuccessful, full of glory or full of worry, but do they *mean* anything? The famous Swiss psychologist Carl Jung observed from his years of practice that many of his patients were not clinically ill or neurotic but suffered from an emptiness and a lack of meaning. According to Jung, "the central neurosis of our time is emptiness." In the play *Death of a Salesman*, Willy Loman examines his many lonely years of existence and concludes that life is meaningless.

When we know what we are supposed to do with our lives and are willing to work hard, we then have a sense of well-being and satisfaction from accomplishing something worthwhile. Meeting this basic need provides significance in a man's life. Many are able to meet this need with a job, church service, or some form of public service. In short, we need to feel that what we do in life is important.

In his book *Man's Search for Meaning*, Victor Frankl records the emotions and behavior of human beings under the most extreme circumstances imaginable.[4] Millions of innocent civilians were forced into Adolf Hitler's concentration camps. Not everyone arrested under Hitler's regime was sent to the gas chambers. Some languished in camps under unspeakable conditions. In the ghastly environment of concentration camps, Frankl noted that while some gave up and died, others persisted, clinging to life despite the outward circumstances.

Frankl found the survivors usually had several things in common that sustained their will to live. The survivors had a purpose for living. Life had meaning. There were loved ones somewhere they wanted to see again. They did not succumb to the feeling that they had been abandoned by either God or people they loved. These individuals had a responsibility to others beyond themselves—they were needed!

Kushner's findings support Frankl's. Concerning innocent civilians in Hitler's camps, Kushner concludes: "Those prisoners whose sense of self depended on their wealth, their social position, their prestigious jobs tended to fall apart when those things were taken away from them. The prisoners whose sense of self grew out of their religious faith or their own self-esteem, rather than other people's opinions of them, tended to fare much better."[5]

Joy comes to our lives when we have three integral ingredients—something to do, someone to love, and something to hope for. When you have something important to do, someone to love, along with hopes and dreams for the future, you are prepared to enjoy the present and anticipate the future.

"Those who have a 'why' for living can handle the 'whats'," wrote Friedrich Nietzsche. Life must have meaning. When it doesn't we are capable of strange, unexplainable, even self-destructive behavior.

Freedom from Obsessive Fear and Guilt

Regret about how we occasionally behave and think is normal. But some people become so obsessed and handicapped with guilt that they fail to function normally. Fear and even guilt have their benefits, but in noncrippling doses. Fear can help us protect ourselves or motivate us to do what we know we should. Dr. Karl Menninger, in his excellent book *Whatever Became of Sin?*, argues that we need certain forms of fear and guilt to help motivate us to do what is right. But negative, obsessive, unconscious fears can cripple the expressions of personality.

In speaking of irrational fears, psychologist Sol Gordon says, "They distort reality, create illusions, and destroy our capacity to deal with the outside world." On the most simple level it can be demonstrated that a person who is intensely afraid literally can't recognize a straight line as being straight. Some people show an exaggerated, unmotivated sense of apprehension in regard to most of the experiences of life.

A woman who worked in a real estate office on the north side of Chicago was such a person. She was always fearful of what people thought, friends and strangers alike. So she selected her clothes, chose her words, and behaved on the basis of what she thought was acceptable to outsiders. When I taught psychology, I would refer to this type of condition as the "dictatorship of the they." This woman and millions like her are crippled with concerns about what the often nebulous "they" might think instead of living in harmony with their basic values.

Such people are unsure of their own worth. What they need is freedom—freedom from their false fears and guilt. A freedom that's obtained by building a healthy attitude about one's self-worth and abilities. This freedom frequently comes through hard emotional and mental work, requiring a break from the shackles of old perceptions and the grasping of new vistas of self. But close, lasting friendships are virtually impossible apart from this psychological achievement.

Self-Respect

We need to feel good about ourselves. Self-confidence and self-respect are prerequisites for a meaningful life. Our feelings about ourselves are developed during relationships with other people.

A college student was home for Christmas vacation. He told his mother he needed to spend time with his father. Father and son went to the family room and talked for more than two hours. Alone they talked about life, women, careers, grades, and the future. Later the mother asked, "What did he want?" The father proudly responded, "Me."

Striving to feel good about yourself is not self-preoccupation or narcissism. You must feel good about yourself or you'll be incapacitated emotionally and relationally. The biblical admonition to "love your neighbor as yourself" (Mark 12:31) is built on this fact. John Powell, author of *The Secret of Staying in Love*, argues that all psychological problems, from a mild neurosis to the deepest psychosis, are symptomatic of the frustration of this fundamental human need for a healthy sense of self-respect.[6]

Understanding

The basic human need of understanding has two sides. Each individual needs to have his attitudes, beliefs, and ideas understood by others. We need people to understand us. Conversely we need to experience and understand deeply the attitudes and feelings of others. To accomplish this interaction requires in-depth communication in which empathy is expressed.

Two great founders of our nation had different views which strained their relationship to the breaking point.

For many years they did not speak. Then in 1816 a letter came to Thomas Jefferson penned from his old adversary, John Adams. The unexpected letter began, "You and I ought not to die before we have explained ourselves to each other." The letter was well received and Jefferson responded quickly with a kind letter of his own. Their resulting correspondence is a rich contribution to American history. As life drew to a close, both men felt the basic need to understand and to be understood.

Larry Crabb says, "When issues that really matter are actually talked about, then there is potential for life changing fellowship." Crabb argues that in good relationships we actually have a responsibility "to give feedback lovingly and to receive feedback non-defensively."[7]

We can tolerate stress and live lives more fully when at least one other person understands our struggles. As we conclude this chapter, it is important to emphasize that these needs are basic and a prerequisite for leading a normal life. To want these needs met is no more selfish than to want food and water for your body or spiritual food for your soul.

DISCUSSION QUESTIONS

1. Why do we often focus on our differences when there exist many human similarities which could unite us?
2. How can we best overcome, or at least minimize, our focus on differences?
3. One of our most profound needs is for human intimacy. How can friendships meet this need in the areas of giving and receiving?
4. How does our self-respect—the way we feel about ourselves—contribute to our ability to form successful relationships with others?

CHAPTER FIVE

What's the Difference?

Male and female He created them.
—Genesis 1:27

Women are different from men—and God wanted it that way. God deliberately created both male and female.

Women make friends more easily than men. They form and sustain relationships at a more qualitative level than do men. Psychologist Elaine Sachnoff concludes from research that friendship means more to women than to men. Their relationships tend to be more meaningful, more satisfying, and of longer duration.

The two assumptions—that the sexes differ and that women have more satisfying friendships than men—are truths that require little validation. But here the agreement ends. The difficult questions we need to face are: How do the sexes differ? Does *maleness* or *femaleness* affect the making and nurturing of relationships with other humans? Do the differences affect our ability to form friendships? Can we as men blame sex differences for being generally friendless? Must *male-*

55

ness somehow hinder a man from forming and sustaining close relationships with other men? The explorations of these questions will help us better understand both our limitations and our potentials as men.

Sexual differences are facts of nature which cannot be minimized or ignored. Many are too obvious to even mention. Much of the recent research dealing with the sexes has been conducted in an attempt to prove that females are not inferior to males. Therefore, there has been a distinct tendency to minimize the differences both in scientific and popular literature. But if we don't take the time to understand the differences, we'll be at a disadvantage when we try to understand and form friendships. So let's look at the differences and see what difference they make.

Physical Differences

Despite the claims of some people, the sexes really are different. In a survey of the literature on sex differences, Dr. David McClelland of Harvard concludes that literally thousands of studies show that significant sex differences do indeed exist. In all human societies men are larger and stronger than women. The average man is 6 percent taller than the average woman. Also, men average about 20 percent more weight than women. The greater body bulk of the male comes mainly from larger muscles and bones. Large muscles in males permit them to lift more weight, throw a ball farther, or run faster than most women. Even at birth the male has more strength to lift his head higher and for longer periods of time than does a female. At puberty the difference in muscle strength is accentuated, largely due to testosterone.

Men have a higher metabolic rate and produce more physical energy than women and thus need more food to keep the body performing to its full potential. Women are usually a few degrees cooler than men and may therefore require less food to maintain a constant weight. Men's blood is richer than women's with an average of three hundred thousand more red corpuscles per cubic millimeter.

With statistics like these, it's understandable why many have concluded that men are physically superior to women. Even some scientists who should know better have fallen for the male superiority myth. Not too surprisingly most of these scientists have been men. For example, Lester Ward, a founding father of American sociology, stated a few decades ago that women were cautious and more conservative than men because of their biological helplessness. Contemporary sociologists and scientists in more recent years are less willing to express their theories on gender so blatantly.

Research has confirmed, however, that rather than being physically inferior, women actually possess certain biological advantages when compared with men. Dr. Estelle Ramey, an endocrinologist at Georgetown University School of Medicine, believes that women outlive men because they are biologically stronger, not because they lead lives that are less stressful. This generalization fails to consider the lifestyle of American men that we discussed in Chapters 1 and 2. Nevertheless, females enjoy some apparent real physical advantages.

Biological differences are established at conception. It's estimated that between 130 and 150 males are conceived for every 100 females. Conception is probably the male's only fundamental biological advantage. But after the beginning of human life, it's downhill for the male sex. Scientists say that by the time of birth, there are only 106 boys to every 100 girls. Many more male fetuses are miscarried because of spontaneous abortion and death *in utero*.

The United States Bureau of Vital Statistics estimates that 25 percent more boy babies than girl babies are born prematurely. Circulatory and respiratory infection, parasites, and viral and digestive diseases plague boys in higher numbers than girls. In fact, there is rarely a disease or defect which doesn't damage boys more than girls.

During the first year of life the mortality rate among boys is almost one-third higher than among girls. Boys have more genetic defects which contribute to their higher death rate. And as if that were not enough, the female physical advantage goes on throughout life into old age.

Men and women differ in every cell of their bodies. In the nucleus of each body's millions of cells, there is present either an XX chromosome for women or an XY chromosome for men. For centuries husbands have placed on their wives the burden of producing a healthy boy baby. And yet the genetic fact is that if a baby is to be a boy, the father must come up with the Y chromosome, the primary sex determiner.

Each female cell contains the chromatin substance that is absent in male cells. The male nervous system too is different from the woman's, as are other parts of his body. The characteristics listed here, and countless others as well, show that there are real biological differences within our species. This research reflects the biblical truth that God created humans distinctly as male and female. "God created man in His own image; in the image of God He created him; male and female He created them" (Gen. 1:27).

Psychological Differences

If the sexes are different physically, aren't they also different psychologically? And if they are indeed different mentally, how much difference really exists? Unless we are able to believe that mind and body are completely separate realms, we should expect psychological as well as the more obvious physical differences between the sexes. As you might imagine, this topic is fraught with controversy and confusion which will not be resolved in the brief discussion here.

People tend to line up with one extreme or the other on this psychological issue as they do on the biological. One group claims that men and women are totally different mentally. For example, they say that women are religious, men are not; women are gentle, men are rough; men are independent, women need security; women talk a great deal, while men talk very little; women appreciate the arts and literature, men do not; women need to care for children, men do not; men need goals and accomplishments, women do not. And the list of stereotypes goes on.

This group maintains that heredity makes men and women completely different not only physically but also in the way we think and behave. Many of the men who hold this view are chauvinists who have acquired a stereotype of what women are like. Some chauvinists are also playboys who view women as possessions or solely as objects of sexual pleasure. The playboy mentality maintains that the ideal woman has a small brain and large breasts.

Well-meaning Christians or even pastors can also adhere to a chauvinistic view of the sexes. Many popular books and sermons that deal with family living discuss *the* role of men and *the* role of women. For example, many people emphasize that the Bible says wives should "submit to" their husbands (Eph. 5:22). But did you know that the Scripture also demands that husbands submit to their wives? In the verse prior to the frequently cited Ephesians 5:22, you find, "Submit to one another out of reverence for Christ" (v. 21). Submission is not for wives only.

To submit is to pay less attention to yourself and more to

your spouse. Submission is the putting aside of your own rights so you can better serve the one you love. Submission implies a conciliatory mindset. Webster's dictionary says to conciliate is "to gain by pleasing acts; to become friendly or agreeable." Submission is not an act of blind obedience but rather an expressed concern for your spouse even at the expense of your own personal desires. Submission is not a male or female issue. It is a biblical and human principle about relationships. We rarely hear this fact, even in the church, because we are locked in a culture that does not view submission as a manly trait.

At the other extreme, a group contends that there really are no psychological or mental differences between the sexes. Men and women are said to have the same abilities and to perform or behave in exactly the same fashion if given the same chances and the same early educational experiences. Many feminists maintain that all differences are culturally determined and have nothing to do with heredity. They say that the typical woman acts like she does because she was taught to act in a certain fashion by parents, teachers, and society, not because it's a true expression of her womanhood.

In the 1930s Dr. Margaret Mead studied the differences in male and female behavior in three tribes of New Guinea. She argued that sex roles are different in different areas of the world and thus concluded that we have no basis for linking one's sex with one's behavior or attitude.[1]

I had an opportunity to talk with Dr. Mead about the topic of sex differences during an anthropology conference many years ago. Our meeting took place shortly before she died. She seemed to have changed her published views somewhat, or at least held them with less vigor. She doubted some of her earlier conclusions, believing that there might exist innate psychological differences between the sexes, but she was unwilling to speculate on which traits might be either learned or innate.

What Is Male? What Is Female?

Both views of the psychological traits of the sexes—that they are completely innate or totally learned—are largely mythical. Both of these extremes need to be avoided. There really are differences, but they are not as extensive as some would like us to believe. *There is substantial evidence that men and women exhibit similar behavior and in some areas manifest different behavior.* Widespread agreement exists among scientists on this. The following statements contain many of their agreements related to sex differences. Note that of all the hundreds of possible behaviors, only a handful are listed either largely male or female in characteristics. Also observe that the first trait is directly related to the formation of friendships.

- Women are more likely than men to express their emotions and display empathy and compassion in response to the emotions of others.
- Men as a whole are more skillful than women at visually perceiving the spatial, or geometric, features of objects. A typical test of their ability involves matching a drawing of an object with the correct drawing of the object from another angle, or as it would be if rotated in space.
- Girls score higher than boys on tests of verbal ability, such as comprehension and production of language, analogies, and spelling. Most evidence shows that this difference appears during adolescence and widens at least through high school.
- A similar developmental difference holds for mathematical abilities, except that in this case boys achieve the higher scores. This may be a result of boys' superior visual/spatial ability, a capacity useful in solving some mathematical problems.
- Females tend to be more anxious than males about

risking failure. When females do fail, they are more likely to blame themselves. When males fail, they tend to blame others.

- Boys tend to be more physically active than girls, doing more running and jumping. At play they range farther than do girls.[2]

Aside from such differences, I believe that very few God-ordained differences exist between the sexes. Therefore there is much room for men to acquire traits which will lead them to more satisfying relationships with other men. Yes, women are more likely than men to express emotions and reveal empathy and compassion, but nothing exists in Scripture or biology that says this is the natural order of things. Therefore, despite our current cultural conditioning that the expression of emotions, including compassion and empathy, are largely female traits, it doesn't have to be this way. Men can learn these traits too.

A Lou Harris survey revealed that women live longer than men at least partially because they practice healthier lifestyles. The survey of 1,250 adults revealed that men are:

- 10 percent less likely than women to limit salt in their diet
- 14 percent less likely to limit fat
- 14 percent less likely to eat plenty of fiber
- 15 percent less likely to limit cholesterol
- 17 percent less likely to obey the speed limit
- 19 percent more likely to drive after drinking
- 12 percent more likely to drink too much
- 8 percent less likely to wear safety belts and take steps to avoid home accidents.[3]

* * *

Researcher Michael Lafavore concludes that 'women just try harder to live longer." This sounds like bad news for men. But men can benefit when they see that longevity is somewhat controllable.

We're capable of more diverse behavior than we might realize. For example, cleaning dishes may be viewed as a woman's job, but this idea comes from our culture, certainly not from the Bible. In fact, 2 Kings 21:13 (KJV) talks about a man wiping dishes. Certain tasks in our society such as changing diapers, mowing the lawn, grocery shopping, driving the kids to school, managing the checkbook, and housecleaning are said to be either woman's work or man's work. All of this role fixation is cultural rather than biologically determined or biblically justifiable.

In our home my wife and I, and our children too, do the housecleaning together. We call this activity "dummy time," I guess because no one really wants to do it. But working together can be fun and the time spent in "dummy time" is over much sooner when more than one person works at it. The point is that family members should think of others within the family when work needs to be done instead of wasting time trying to decide which job is for males and which is for females.

One man, following his wife's request that he help with the housework, remarked sarcastically, "That's not my job. The next thing I know you'll be asking me to wear dresses and use perfume and makeup. I'm a man. Don't you realize that?" Actually we can find historical illustrations when wigs, bloomers, long stockings, lace blouses, and high heels were worn by men and considered manly in the time period in which they appeared. During America's colonial period, many of these items were popular with men.

The late columnist Sydney Harris expressed his irrita-

tion with our culture's narrow and distorted definition of
manliness:

> As I was edging out of a parking lot the other day, some
> Clyde in his Bonneville cut sharply ahead of me, flashed a
> sour smile of triumph in my direction, and scooted away.
> He thought he was displaying strength and aggressive-
> ness; I thought he was displaying weakness and bad man-
> ners.
>
> What the prevailing ethos in modern American life
> does not seem to understand is that true strength always
> reveals itself in gentleness and courtesy; this was the whole
> medieval idea of knighthood and chivalry—a knight was
> chivalrous because he felt strong enough to afford it.
>
> We tend to confuse rudeness with power and aggres-
> siveness with virility. Many, if not most, of the bad-
> mannered drivers on the road are slack-jawed youths who
> privately feel weak and insecure in their personal relations
> with the world; tooling a ferocious car gives them a vicari-
> ous sense of power they do not possess in person.
>
> Genuine strength of character is always accompanied
> by a feeling of security that allows one to practice civility
> and courtesy—but, in our perverse culture, civility and
> courtesy are often regarded as signs of weakness or some
> lack of "manliness."
>
> And it is largely this perverse evaluation of what consti-
> tutes manhood that accounts for so much of the dangerous
> discourtesy on our nation's highways—somehow, the edu-
> cation of boys here has stressed aggressiveness at the price
> of gentleness, so that many youths act like boors in order to
> be thought of as "men."
>
> This is fairly indigenous to our culture; in other coun-
> tries, a more balanced view is taken of what comprises
> "manliness," and one of the main criteria of an adult male
> is his considerateness for others. And the poor result of our
> misconception of manhood can be seen in many failing
> marriages, where the wives uniformly complain that their
> husbands are just "little boys who failed to grow up."[4]

Our definition of manliness or masculinity *is* too narrow and usually distorted. We see ourselves and women as opposites; we even use the phrase "the opposite sex." But we're not opposite; we are, however, different. Remember, of the forty-eight chromosomes in each human cell, only one relates to sex.

The Biblical Perspective

Throughout history, most people, including Christians, have assumed that a proper interpretation of Genesis 1:27 meant that any and all differences in their society between males and females existed because God created these differences, not because they had been learned within their culture.

With the emergence of the social and behavioral sciences, we have begun to question the "absolute role" which biology plays in the formation of sexual temperament and behavior. *"Culture," rather than "nature," is the major influence in determining the temperamental differences between the sexes.* In other words, we are more alike than we previously realized. Following the Great Depression, women began in large numbers to enter the work force, and in the early 1990s, the majority of women are working outside the home. Men today are more likely to help with children and with domestic tasks that historically have been considered woman's work. So much for the 1950s Ozzie and Harriet stereotype of the husband as sole provider and the wife as the nonemployed partner who cares for the kids and prepares meals.

It is incorrect for Christians to assume that the particular definition of masculinity and femininity learned in their culture is God's definition. It is inaccurate to hold this ethnocentric view of the world. We fall into this trap by reading our cultural expectations into Scripture. When the Bible comments on basic human traits, it doesn't distinguish between the sexes. For example, in the Sermon on the Mount, the Lord calls those blessed who are sorrowful, who possess a gentle spirit, who show mercy, whose hearts are pure, and who are peaceful. The same is true of the spiritual gifts; the apostle Paul did not list any of them with gender tags (1 Cor. 12).

This is good news! You're more malleable than you may have realized. Sure, you're a man, but that doesn't mean you cannot learn to be a compassionate, courteous, loving, listening, caring human being if you're presently lacking any of these characteristics. In other words, *if you don't now have the traits for developing friendships, you can acquire them.*

It is wrong to argue that women are genetically different from men in friendship capacities. If women acquire and maintain friendships better than men—and they do—men are free to acquire the characteristics that women possess.

I have no intention of minimizing the distinctions between the sexes. They are real and they are good. But we must remember that men and women are more alike than we might realize. So if you're caught in some limited male role that you have attributed to your maleness, remember that your behavior may actually be the result of social learning rather than your biological or temperamental maleness.

How can you determine if an aspect of your personality is the product of nature or social conditioning? Use the following test. Ask yourself: Is this aspect of my personality a positive attribute or is it destructive? If a certain behavior hinders the formation of friendships, it should be viewed not as masculine but as destructive. If behavior encourages friendship formation, view this behavior as positive, not feminine.

The great thing about learned negative behavior is that you can unlearn it and thus gain a fresh start. For years a woman cut off both ends of a ham before cooking it. Her inquisitive young daughter asked, "Why do you cut off each end, Mom?" The response, "I don't really know. I've always done it that way. I guess I learned it from your grandmother." Undaunted, the little girl asked her grandmother why both she and Mother "cut off the ends." Grandmother was surprised to learn that this had become a family tradition. "Honey," she said, "I had to cut off the ends because the ham wouldn't fit in my small roasting pan."

You may laugh at this story but don't miss its message. We have learned many things in life, and what we have learned contributes to the way we currently live our lives. Some of what we have learned, like the lady who still hacks off the ends of the ham, is unnecessary but harmless. We have also acquired, from earlier learning, much that is positive and good. But some aspects of our early training are cultural baggage that we should dispose of. Much of this destructive learning results from a narrow and incorrect view of what constitutes manliness.

Our God-given maleness need not be a social handicap and should not be used by us to defend a friendless existence. A man told me, "Of course I don't have friends. I'm a man. My wife is the one with the friends." His implication was that his friendless condition was part of his genetic rather than his social background. Our biological maleness is not a barrier to developing relationships, and social barriers can be unlearned.

It has been said that we are all self-made, but only the rich admit it. If we are not happy with our situation, we can change it. Only our resistance to change prevents us from cultivating the warm, meaningful relationships enjoyed by many women and a handful of other men.

DISCUSSION QUESTIONS

1. Do you believe that being a man should in any way affect your ability to make quality friendships? Why? Why not?
2. In what ways has our culture provided definitions of what it means to be male that are in conflict with either the Bible or scientific research?
3. We use the term "opposite sex." What other terms would be more accurate?
4. What aspects of your personality that may be destructive can you change? What roles might prayer and commitment play?

CHAPTER SIX

Biblical Principles
of Friendship

You have made known to me the path of life.
—Psalm 16:11

Many men may not recognize the true nature of friendship, mistaking it for various counterfeits. Fortunately, the Bible offers examples and principles for us to learn to apply in our own lives.

Perhaps the greatest biblical example of two men in close fellowship is the relationship between David and Jonathan. Their unity is mentioned in 1 Samuel 18:1, "the soul of Jonathan was knit to the soul of David" (RSV).

Jonathan was the oldest son of Saul, the first king of the nation of Israel. Jonathan had many great military victories over various enemies of Israel, but he is remembered not so much for his military wisdom and bravery as for being the friend of David. David became Israel's greatest king and one of the most important individuals in all of Israel's history.

The two men met shortly after David's successful encounter with the Philistine, Goliath. David and Jonathan's love for each other began the day they **69** met and continued over time, despite social class differences. Jonathan's father also hindered the friendship in that he tried on several occasions to kill David. Jonathan more than once risked his own life for David. On one occasion, Saul was angry because Jonathan did not share his hostile view of David. Unable to control his emotions, Saul actually threw a spear at his own son. Despite the unpredictable harassment and danger, Jonathan remained committed to his friend David. And David, despite the dangers of secretly meeting with the king's son, remained loyal to Jonathan.

For a biblical example of what not to do in a friendship, we can turn to what is probably the oldest book in the Bible—Job. This great section of Scripture illustrates that, despite circumstances, man has the capacity for a faith completely centered on God.

Job lost his health, his children, and much that he owned. He lost the support of his friends, and his wife was impatient with his tragic circumstances, advising him to "curse God and die." Job's multiple sufferings were compounded not just with a lack of sympathy but with overt emotional harassment and condemnation by his three so-called friends. Zophar, Eliphaz, and Bildad told Job he must have committed some gross sin for all these calamities to befall him. *Why else would he be suffering so much?* they reasoned.

Eliphaz summed up their thinking when he asked Job a rhetorical question: "Remember now, who ever perished being innocent? Or where were the upright ever cut off?" Eliphaz continued without waiting for Job's response. "Even as I have seen, those who plow iniquity and sow trouble reap the same" (4:7–8). You can almost hear the judgmental and self-righteous tone of this man's voice as you read the passage. The fact is, these pseudo-friends, with their criticism and self-righteousness, failed to look at Job's pain from a different point of view. They reached the easy but wrong conclusion that God must be punishing Job for some unrevealed sin.

If we had to choose a friendship like that between David and Jonathan or that of Job and his crew, we would all prefer the kindness and commitment that existed between David and Jonathan. But close friendships don't just happen. They result from the application of principles recorded throughout the Word of God.

While preparing to write this book, I read through the Bible with the specific purpose of finding rules or principles for friendship. I was at first surprised to learn that God has so much to say about this topic. We tend to think of the Bible as a book of personal redemption, which is true, but the Bible also includes a great deal about our relationships with other people. In fact, the Bible touches upon every kind of human relationship, including friendship.

The Bible places emphasis upon six principles of friendship. These basic themes keep appearing in different examples throughout Scripture. In the following survey of these six principles, we will learn what spiritual and/or personality traits need to be either added to or deleted from our personal lives.

Principle 1: God-Centered Basis of Belief

Today's Christian believes, as the Westminster Shorter Catechism recorded in 1793, that "man's chief end is to glorify God and to enjoy Him forever." *Intimate friendships rarely develop when individuals do not share at least a basic consensus of beliefs.*

In Psalm 1:1 we read that "Blessed is the man who walks not in the counsel of the ungodly." Second Corinthians 6:14 states, "Do not be unequally yoked together with unbelievers." Two men with the same biblical value system can seek each other's counsel with confidence that the responses will be based on Scripture. David, for example, came to Jonathan for counsel (1 Sam. 20), knowing the advice would be sound. Moses accepted the advice of Jethro (Ex. 18:13–27), as Timothy did of Paul (1 Tim. 6:11–16; 2 Tim. 3:10–17).

Author Jerry Jenkins says, "At times I need to let my hair down, tell somebody everything, revert to adolescence and enjoy a relationship built on years of trust and confidence."[1] Usually we have this kind of openness only with people with whom we share core values, but this is not always true.

I have a few friends who do not share my religious faith or political beliefs. John and I were in graduate school together in the late 1960s. Our ideas are often different, but we share a respect for each other and each other's views. Despite our differences we have maintained a friendship throughout the years, largely because of this mutual respect. The friendship I have with John is a good one, but I think it is rare. Most close friends share the same faith and virtually the same value system.

Principle 2: Formation of Covenant

"And Jonathan made a covenant with David because he loved him as himself" (1 Sam. 18:3).

Virtually every important relationship or event in our society is acknowledged with ritual and ceremony in the presence of others. Marriage is the best illustration of this. The couple is formally recognized by relatives, friends, the church, and even the legal structure. Recognition marks what anthropologists call "rites of passage." Rites occur at birth, baptism, graduation, club initiations, and death. These and other transitions are accompanied by some formal ritual that signifies the passing from one stage of life into another. Through ceremony we recognize that which we regard with honor.

After an individual has received God's love by accepting Christ as Savior, most evangelical churches ask for public profession of the conversion. In Romans 10:9–10, Paul wrote about the need for a public profession. The congregation witnesses and acknowledges the new believer's expression of faith.

The significant events in our lives should include ceremony. Despite what many young and some older people believe, we do need rituals in our lives. In the musical *Fiddler on the Roof*, Tevya sings of his strong belief in rituals and traditions. Social science research supports the need for the formation of covenants which are witnessed by others. They help provide meaning, acceptance of transition, recognition, and encouragement for ourselves and others. Covenants tell the world that the action we have taken is important.

In America the important relationship of friendship is devoid of any type of ceremony and covenant formation. When we decide to commit to a friendship, rarely is there a public testimony or occasion for acknowledgment by family and other friends.

The Bible, however, encourages the establishment of a covenant when men become friends. Jonathan and David, because of their mutual love, decided to make a covenant. A covenant is a promise, a contract, a binding agreement, a formation of unity. "The soul of Jonathan was knit to the soul of David." *Knit*, a term which means "to unite," is the same word used in Genesis to express Jacob's love for his youngest son, Benjamin (Gen. 35:18).

To show outwardly his inward love, Jonathan took off his robe, tunic, sword, bow, and belt and gave them all to his dear friend, David. This symbolic gesture, this outward expression of Jonathan's love, affected greatly their commitment to each other. David, being a peasant and therefore not wealthy, could return only the gift of loyalty and respect to his friend.

The giving and accepting of a tangible token to represent commitment helps solidify friendships like the exchanging of rings during a wedding ceremony. Friends can give modest gifts and remember important days and anniversaries with cards, calls, and letters. These expressions of our friendship should be thoughtful, personal, and creative. I still use the pencil sharpener a friend gave me when I entered college. I still smile when I think of the friend who gave me a sapling for my birthday. He knew I wanted more shade in the backyard of our home.

The gifts are appreciated but it is the giver, the one who thought of me, that I cherish. The commitment of the friend and the covenant between us has been marked by the gift. It is vital that friends know that we care about them personally. The very least we can do is tell them how highly we value them and our relationship with them. In short, we should form covenants with friends.

Principle 3: Faithfulness

There are few things more irritating than someone who is unpredictable and cannot be counted on when you really need him. In Proverbs 14:20 and 19:4, we read that wealth adds many friends. These fair-weather friends may be plentiful, but they are not worth very much. The writer of Proverbs says that a true friend "sticks closer than a brother" (18:24), and we are admonished, "Do not forsake your friend" (27:10).

While the world's philosophy tends to be "Laugh and the world laughs with you, cry and you cry alone," biblical friendship calls for faithfulness. Circumstances should not affect our consistency. In Romans 12:15 Paul tells us to "rejoice with those who rejoice," and to "weep with those who weep" (RSV).

I'm reminded of Job's three friends when I read Proverbs 25:19, "Trust in a faithless man in time of trouble is like a bad tooth or a foot that slips" (RSV). This is, to say the least, a rather graphic illustration of the grief one can suffer from an unfaithful friend.

Unfaithfulness often rears its ugly head at times when we are most vulnerable. Sickness, unemployment, or poverty can quickly thin the ranks of friends. A popular young man I know quite well went through a painful divorce. I was very surprised, for Carl and his wife seemed to be the "model couple." Carl's wife fell for the attention and charm of her influential boss. Everyone in Carl's closely knit neighborhood was surprised by the affair. Carl was shocked and devastated. During and following the divorce, he needed the companionship and support of his friends. And yet at this time in his life when he needed them most, some of his friends began to give him the cold shoulder. How could this happen?

So much of our social lives is structured in couple-oriented activities, and Carl was no longer part of his old married neighborhood group. I think the rejection may have gone deeper, however. Carl was now an unattached, rather handsome man who was perceived, not as a lonely grief-stricken person who needed his neighborhood friends during a difficult period, but rather as a threat. *Who knows? Maybe he'll try to steal my wife*, may have been the conscious or unconscious reasoning on the part of the men who abandoned him in his time of need. The insecurities of these men prevented them from being faithful to a friend.

Faithfulness is critical to a close relationship because we depend on those who are close to us. Christ's deepest hurts occurred within his circle of closest companions, and David was wounded emotionally more by the treachery of his close friends than by the efforts of his enemies. He laments in Psalm 55:12–14, "If an enemy were insulting me, I could endure it; if a foe were raising himself against me, I could hide from him. But it is you, a man like myself, my companion, my close friend, with whom I once enjoyed sweet fellowship as we walked with the throng at the house of God" (NIV). Paul too was left to stand alone when he was deserted by Demas and others (2 Tim. 4:10).

A faithful friend keeps confidences. Again in Proverbs we read that "a perverse man stirs up dissension and a gossip separates close friends" (16:28). And in 17:9, "He who covers over an offense promotes love, but whoever repeats the matter separates close friends."

Entering friendship involves revealing yourself in confidence to another, and thus becoming vulnerable. This is as it should be, but it is what makes betrayal so evil and faithfulness so virtuous.

Principle 4: Social Involvement

In our highly mobile society where approximately 20 percent of our population move annually, few men are willing to form lasting commitments to a community or to individuals. And yet Scripture admonishes us to be good neighbors, involved in the lives of others. Being good neighbors is a form of friendship.

A good neighbor or friend is not only reluctant to start trouble (Prov. 3:29) but also unwilling to spread it (Prov. 25:8,9). Silence is better than criticism. When I was a boy of ten or eleven, my father told me, "If you can't say something good about somebody, don't say anything at all." So often when we spread unflattering or even untruthful statements, we really tell others more about our own character than we do of the person we are condemning. In fact, the Bible says that the man who "does not bridle his tongue, . . . deceives his own heart, this one's religion is useless" (James 1:26).

"He who despises his neighbor sins; But he who has mercy on the poor, happy is he" (Prov. 14:21). When Christ was asked by a lawyer, "Who is my neighbor?", the Lord responded with the parable of the good Samaritan. A man was going from Jerusalem to Jericho when he was robbed and beaten. The thieves left him to die. A priest and later a Levite traveled past the victim but refused to get involved. Lacking basic human compassion, these two leaders went by, leaving the man to die. The next man on the scene was a Samaritan. The Samaritans were the social outcasts of Jesus' day, similar to the untouchables of India. This man, the Samaritan, cared for the victim's wounds and took him to a local boardinghouse to recuperate. He paid an innkeeper for the night and promised to pay for all the victim's expenses until he was well enough to travel.

Referring to the Samaritan, Jesus said, "Go and do likewise" (Luke 10:29–37). We are required to get involved in the lives of others.

However, the lessons from Jesus and the Proverbs should not leave the impression that we must attempt involvement with anyone and everyone. We are to keep our distance from some. Involvement is not indiscriminate, for the Bible says, "Do not make friends with a hot-tempered man, do not associate with one easily angered" (Prov. 22:24). The psalmist also warns that we not fellowship with the wicked.

We may sometimes avoid people who act or think differently from us and defend our lack of social and spiritual involvement by appealing to the wicked-neighbor argument. But that's a misuse of the biblical admonition just cited. In point of fact, most people we meet will respond favorably to kindness and cordiality if we take the time and trouble to find a common interest. In the mid-sixties in a suburban Chicago church, I was working with boys in a youth group. One evening while making home visits, I met a man who was angry that I had interrupted his favorite TV show. What followed were a few anxious moments, but when he realized that I was concerned about his son, he changed his attitude markedly. Our conversation improved. A few weeks later he began attending the church on a regular basis. Despite our differences—and they were many—we were able to get along because we at first found an area of common interest, his son.

Along with their wives, married men should take responsibility in social relationships. Too often men do very little to make or maintain social contact with others. Usually the entire enterprise is left to the wife. It is the wife who schedules social engagements and handles details about children and other family concerns. And if friends move away, the wife rather than the husband writes letters and sends gifts to maintain the relationship.

I well remember an exception to this generalization. Several years ago following a family move, we began the sometimes pleasant (other times unpleasant) task of hunting for a church. In one church a man introduced himself to me and we had a good talk. Paul took a personal interest in me. Without being nosey he was genuinely interested in me as a person. A couple of Sundays later Paul asked my wife and me to join his family for lunch following the worship hour. A few weeks later he asked if I would like to help him lead a large Sunday School discussion group on the Gospel of Mark. We worked on the lessons while having early breakfast together once or twice a month. I'm sure our family would have joined this particular church even if Paul had not taken such a special interest in me. But I'm glad he did.

Three years later I was asked by the church nominating committee to serve as chairman of the church. I told the committee that I would need time to think, study, and pray about this request. In my prayers I expressed the gut feeling that I was unqualified for the position. This feeling seemed to be reinforced as I studied the third chapter of 1 Timothy, the first chapter of Titus, and other related passages.

I sought the counsel of my friend Paul. He helped me see that my respect for the chairman's role, along with my feelings of unworthiness, were actually traits that a church leader should possess. He told me I should seek the Lord's guidance rather than depend exclusively upon my own strength and reasoning. Partially due to this man's support and confidence, I accepted the chairmanship.

It's important for us to reach out to other men with the investment of our time and concern. We have a responsibility to involve ourselves with other men. And when we fulfill that obligation, we and the men we befriend will benefit.

Principle 5: Candor

Two verses from Proverbs support this principle. "Faithful are the wounds of a friend" (27:6). "Reproof is more effective for a wise man" (17:10).

Give it to me straight. What do you really think? Is the friend who will level with you or even rebuke you better than one who is insincere or speaks false words of affection?

The incisive words of a true friend may hurt your pride and feelings at the moment, but over the long haul you'll be better off for having heard them. By contrast, the flattery or neglect of a false friend can bring you harm in the long run (see Prov. 29:5). Refusing to speak rebuke can also bring harm. David neglected his duty to his son Adonijah and it ultimately cost that son his life (1 Kings 1:6).

A friend will help you face the truth even if you don't want to hear it at the moment. The candor of a friend can provide the perspective or point of view you need to make wise decisions.

I believe the majority of people feel that arguments are destructive to a relationship and, therefore, differences of opinion should be kept to oneself. This is not necessarily true. Expressing differences does not mean that we do not respect the feelings of others. Actually, we tend to keep our feelings from those people who are only our acquaintances, not our close friends. This is also true of differences of opinion. "As iron sharpens iron, so a man sharpens the countenance of his friend" (Prov. 27:17). We learn and grow when we listen to different ideas.

A close friend, seeing a need, a personality flaw, or a problem will not remain quiet, even when doing so appears prudent. When Moses was struggling to create a legal social order for the nation of Israel, his father-in-law, Jethro, said, "Listen now to my voice; I will give you counsel" (Ex. 18:19). Moses was exhausted trying to settle every dispute the people could manufacture. Jethro told Moses his work load was too heavy and suggested that he teach others to be fair judges, thus speeding up the resolution of disputes.

It would have been easier for Jethro to stay out of it. Why take the risk of being ridiculed or accused of meddling or be embarrassed if Moses refused the advice? But Jethro cared for Moses and the nation of Israel and was therefore willing to be candid, and Moses listened and did as his father-in-law suggested.

The willingness to express your own needs to friends is another aspect of this principle of candor. Paul the apostle, after converting a slave to the Lord, sent him back to his master, Philemon of Colossae. The slave Onesimus carried a letter from Paul in which he told Philemon to welcome this slave as he would welcome Paul (Philem. 17). Paul asked Philemon to receive Onesimus as a brother and reminded him in the short letter that Philemon was indebted to him and Paul wanted him to do this favor.

In Matthew 16 Jesus asked the disciples what the people were saying about him. In response a few of his followers gave him some safe and noncommittal answers. He then gave them a rather candid question: "But who do you say that I am?" (v. 15). Perhaps there was a long silence. Then the impulsive but devoted Peter replied, "You are the Christ, the Son of the living God" (v. 16). Peter left no doubt about his perception of Jesus. As a friend and follower, he shot straight with Jesus.

Possibly the most candid statement in Scripture is Christ's response to Nicodemus in the third chapter of the Gospel of John. Cautious Nicodemus, a member of the Jewish conservative religious elite, did not want to meet Jesus during the day, so he approached Jesus during the night, while no one could detect his visit. He was interested in Jesus' teachings and miracles, but he did not yet understand that Jesus was the Christ—the long awaited Messiah. With simple curiosity, Nicodemus came to speak with him. The Lord cut right through to the heart of Nicodemus's problem when he said, "I say to you, unless one is born anew, he cannot see the kingdom of God" (v. 3 RSV). Most of the conversations the Lord had with people were very straightforward.

Honest, forthright speech is encouraged by New Testament phrases such as "speaking the truth in love" (Eph. 4:15), "Let your 'Yes,' be 'Yes,' and your 'No,' 'No'" (James

5:12), and "Be angry, and do not sin" (Ps. 4:4). But it must be remembered that candor is derived from our love and concern for another's well-being. And candor is reciprocal; we must be willing to *listen* to our friends' advice to us, not just give it to them.

Candor then, in the biblical sense, means always having the interests and well-being of the other person in mind when you speak.

Principle 6: Respect

The Bible teaches that each individual is a unique creation of Almighty God. Each of us has inherent worth and dignity, not because of what we can do but, simply and yet profoundly, because we were purposefully created by the hand of God. Therefore, we should respect the humanness of each person, realizing that God loves each and every individual.

The American Heritage Dictionary defines the verb *respect* as follows: "to feel or show esteem for, to honor, to show consideration for, avoid violation of, treat with deference." Many people feel that close friends no longer need to show respect or deference to each other. The Bible warns against making such a major mistake.

Proverbs is rich in teachings on the importance of being respectful of close friends. Some people strain a friendship by, for example, outstaying a welcome. If I fail to show respect for my friend's need to be alone or to be with his family or simply to be away from me, I will cause great harm to the relationship. There is truth to the adage "familiarity breeds contempt." We read in Proverbs 25:17, "Seldom set foot in your neighbor's house, lest he become weary of you and hate you." Powerful words, aren't they? One does not show respect when he is thoughtless or takes advantage of an intimate friendship.

A lack of respect will hinder or destroy the best of relationships. Two men I know are no longer close friends because of this issue of respect. They still speak and on occasion will spend an evening together with their wives. But the great love that existed for years between these two has vanished.

I asked each man what had happened. Steve answered, "Bill is cold and aloof. He refuses to take my advice. And besides, his emphasis on material things has affected his love for God." When I asked Bill about this situation, he said that Steve had attempted to invade both his home and his beliefs, violating the principle of mutual respect. "He was unhappy with our middle-class lifestyle and made subtle comments about it. Steve would come to my house with his family, spend the entire weekend, eat my food, allow his kids to make a mess of our home, and finally leave without a word of thanks. The final straw came when he told my wife she was not studying the Bible correctly and should follow his method."

Their responses are sad; with more respect and better communication the rift could have been prevented. The closest of friendships need guarding if they are to be maintained.

An important ingredient in the principle of respect is toleration of individual differences. You must see things from a friend's point of view. And you must give him the time and space and respect to be what God has allowed him to be.

David knew Jonathan was the king's son. He could have viewed him as the heir to the throne of the man who wanted him dead. On the other hand, Jonathan could have viewed David as an aggressive and rebellious peasant who was trying to destroy his father's reign as king of Israel. Neither of these young men resorted to a limited, narrow view of the other. Rather, they embraced each other as total human beings and maintained respect for each other's right to be an individual.

Christ's Example

The best illustration of friendship is given to us in the life of Jesus Christ. His interaction with others provides us with countless examples that we can hold up as our goal for dealing with other men. I recommend that you read with care the words and deeds of Jesus as recorded in the Gospels.

Read how Jesus called his disciples, how he related to others (even his enemies) in love, how he encouraged people to live more holy and caring lives, and what he taught about the unfairness of judging others. He showed his compassion for both crowds and individuals, for adults and for children, and even for those who sinned. He revealed his humanity and vulnerability at Gethsemane. He taught us about giving to others and meeting their physical needs. He taught us how to talk with others who are different from ourselves and how to visit as a guest. He taught us how to be kind and caring. He taught us how to love as a friend.

Remember, it didn't and still doesn't matter to Christ who you are or what your background is. For he loves unconditionally. In 1 John 4:10, John tells us, "In this is love, not that we loved God, but that He loved us and sent His Son to be the propitiation for our sins." John continues with the ultimate challenge, "Beloved, if God so loved us, we also ought to love one another" (v. 11). Paul also, in Romans 5:6–10, comments on Christ's great love.

Our goal, then, is to love others. Indeed, the very mark of the Christian and the command of Christ is that we love one another (John 13:35). Love is at the foundation of each of the biblical principles mentioned in this chapter. Love is at the foundation of all that is meaningful in our relationships with others.

DISCUSSION QUESTIONS

1. Discuss several ways to begin friendships. Do your answers vary depending on the personality of each potential friend or the context in which you meet?
2. Can you list five major obligations you have to each of your friends? What five things should you be able to expect in return?
3. What rituals and/or ceremonies for friendship would you be comfortable with in your personal relationships?
4. What are several dangers in saying, as Jethro did to Moses, "Listen now to me and I will give you some advice"? How can you protect against these dangers and yet practice candor?
5. How do you resolve the dilemma of both respecting the individuality of your friends and yet wanting what's best for them as you see it?

CHAPTER SEVEN

Friendship Qualities We Look for in Others

The porcupine, whom we must handle gloved, may be respected, but is never loved.
                                    —Arthur Guiterman

E ach of us has met hundreds, perhaps thousands, of individuals during our lives. People enter our lives for a moment or perhaps a lifetime. Some we feel close to after a few hours and some we know for years but really never know at all.

Of all the hundreds of people you know, I believe only five or six individuals become the most important people throughout your entire life. These important people may be young or old, rich or poor, influential or unknown, living or dead. And despite significant differences, these few people surface to your consciousness, because they share fundamental characteristics.

Whom do you love and respect deeply? Who has influenced you? Who brings joy and meaning to your life? And what is it about these few precious people that attracts you to them for a lifetime? If someone asked you to describe why you love someone, you wouldn't answer by describing him or her physically. What is it, then, that makes a few individuals very precious to us?

For years I have shared the following informal questions with many people:

1. Who are the five or six most influential people in your life? These are the individuals who have had the most positive influence on your life. List their names and their relationship to you—friend, parent, spouse, teacher, employer, sibling, etc.
2. Why are these individuals so important to you? List the personality and character traits they have that attracted you to them.

Two extra questions are listed for your reflection.

3. Do you have the same traits that you like in others?
4. What trait do you most admire in others that you *do not* have yourself?

Usually the list of individuals includes parents, brothers or sisters, perhaps a teacher, and sometimes close friends. The responses to the second question are often similar, centering on six significant personality qualities: acceptance, empathy, a willingness to listen, loyalty, self-disclosure, and compromise.

These basic human traits can draw men together. Each of the six requires an element of love. They overlap somewhat, but they are useful to consider separately as we discuss friendship qualities. Many of the responses people shared with me were similar to answers given on the friendship survey listed at the beginning of this book.

Acceptance

I remember being a guest on a talk show on which the popular host was someone I had always admired and respected for the values and causes he represented. I did not perform well. I was nervous and tired following a cross-country flight and a sleepless night in a hotel. And despite my attempts to build a bridge of respect and admiration with the host, he was cool and rather formal toward me. After the taping, he quickly left the studio. Even though that incident took place seven years ago, I still feel the hurt of his rejection. We all want and need to be accepted by others whom we value, and we feel pain when acceptance is not forthcoming, even years following the rejection.

A retired man told me that he felt accepted and loved by his wife because "she doesn't hold grudges." He added, "She gets mad at me, sure, but she gets over it in a hurry."

But some people never seem to *forget*—an essential quality in forgiving. Sure, everyone gets angry, but we need to deal with it, not let it stew for long periods.

I read recently a terrific suggestion that we should have an annual Reconciliation Day when we would set aside our anger toward others and seek to make amends.

In Ann Landers' column of March 18, 1989, a story unfolds where two people teach us valuable lessons. A woman opened an envelope she received in the mail and was startled to discover a check for $3,000 and a letter from a Pennsylvania man who had stolen her wallet containing $95 twenty years before. He had adjusted the amount for twenty years of inflation.

In part the letter said, "I stole your wallet. I promised God that I would make restitution and according to the Bible anything stolen should be returned fourfold. I am sorry for any inconvenience I caused your family." The man was ill and confined to a wheelchair. The woman considered returning the money but wisely realized that he needed to be forgiven and this restitution was his way of showing it. In her reply to the man, she wrote, "Everyone makes mistakes at sometime in their lives and we all need to be forgiven."

The Bible warns, "Do not let the sun go down on your wrath (Eph. 4:26). The Ephesian letter continues: "Let all bitterness, wrath, anger, clamor, and evil speaking be put away from you, with all malice. And be kind to one another, tenderhearted, forgiving one another, just as God in Christ also forgave you" (vv. 31,32). To forgive, to let anger subside, is to accept others as humans, capable of making mistakes.

A successful businessman once told me he wanted a divorce because his wife was no longer "interesting" to him. He had an image of what a perfect wife should be, and since his wife failed to measure up, he wanted out. It's no surprise that his wife is a broken woman; she tried hard to measure up, but she failed. She needed acceptance as she was, not as some image of her husband.

We need to get beyond the "I'm right, you're wrong" trap. A better approach is, "We're different; let's accept that." Unity need not mean uniformity. We need to accept one another despite our differences.

Dr. Carl Rogers, the noted psychologist, says that if we want to build relationships, if we want to learn to accept others, we must "destroy the idea of what a person should be." A woman constantly bugged her husband to take out the garbage until he said, "As soon as you stop nagging, I'll take it out." A woman addicted to cigarettes complained to Ann Landers about how her husband nagged her about her habit. "I need his compassion, not his scolding."

Few people change when they're told to, even if it's "for their own good." When we stop trying to change people and simply accept them the way they are—even with their irritating habits—we put people at ease. They feel loved—and surprisingly, are more likely to change. They know that a part of our acceptance is wanting them to improve and to do better. It is a fact of human nature that when we know we are accepted, we are willing to be held responsible. Wisdom is sometimes learning what to overlook.

On my informal surveys, people often say of an accepting friend, "He realizes he's not perfect and I guess that makes him more willing to accept my imperfections." If we admit that we have faults, we're more likely to be sympathetic to the imperfections of others. Matthew's Gospel asks, "Why do you look at the speck in your brother's eye, but do not consider the plank in your own eye?" (7:3).

A boy caught red-handed in mischief by his mother tearfully asked, "Do you love me anyway?" We never outgrow the need for assurance that someone truly unconditionally loves us. The key to close relationships is *being loved anyway*. That's acceptance.

Empathy

An answer on the questionnaire demonstrated the empathy of friendship: "When I have a serious problem my friend asks, 'What are *we* going to do about it?' Can you imagine that I am so lucky as to have a friend who is willing to share problems as well as joys?" The New Testament says we should "rejoice with those who rejoice, weep with those who weep" (Rom. 12:15 RSV).

One man responded on a questionnaire, "Usually I don't like it when someone responds to my grief with 'I know how you feel.' They don't know how I feel." This man was not afraid of a close relationship. He did, however, resent superficiality. Saying the perfunctory words is not being an empathetic friend.

I'm convinced that some of the deepest friendships develop during sorrow. If we shrink from others when they are in need, we miss the opportunity to help, and we miss the chance to build a friendship.

A social worker was teaching an adult Sunday school class in Indianapolis. Bryon and his wife had been close to a married couple who suddenly lost a child in an accident. Bryon went to the funeral home to offer help and sympathy. Instead, he simply broke down and cried. Bryon may have been embarrassed, but his friends will always remember his empathy during their personal crisis.

Nolan and Nathan Lovas of Waukesha, Wisconsin, are identical twins. Years ago when they were seven years old, Nolan developed leukemia. The chemotherapy treatments caused all of his hair to fall out. So that Nolan wouldn't be the only one at school with a bald head, Nathan shaved his head. The twins continued to look identical, even in illness.

During the 1980 presidential primary season, *Newsweek* magazine told this story about George Bush: While a boy in school, the future president was with a group of boys who laughed at a fat youngster stuck in a playground tunnel. Rather than join the laughter, George ran to his side and helped push him through, apparently unconcerned about what the gang might think.

A true friend will come to your aid even if it's unpopular, for he's interested in you. When we are concerned with others, we tend to be less aware of ourselves. It's ironic how happiness eludes those who seek it directly, often in self-indulgence. But the person who takes on the burden of concern for the welfare of others discovers, sometimes surprisingly, that he has obtained happiness.

To be empathetic means to treat people as equals. A retired schoolteacher told me she can often tell if someone has a child's heart by his or her body language. The person who cares will kneel and speak to the little person at his or her level—eye to eye.

While a senior in college, I substitute taught in a third-grade class at Harrison School on the west side of South Bend, Indiana. It was the custom of each student, upon entering the room in the morning, to give twenty-five cents to the teacher to be held until lunchtime.

The first day I pinch-hit for the regular teacher, one of the boys took a quarter out of the desk before we broke for lunch. At lunchtime I was short one quarter. After I found out who had taken the money, I sent the other children on to lunch. Billy had taken the money because he was hungry. He came from a poverty-stricken and broken home and was often sent to school with neither breakfast nor money for lunch. It would have been easy to chastise him; and it was necessary, of course, to help Billy see that it was wrong to take someone else's quarter.

Still, a hungry boy sat before me. The school provided him a lunch that day and began work on getting him into its lunch program.

The next day, the children came in with their books and quarters. I talked with Billy during a break and, while he was surprised, he was eager to pass out the quarters just before lunch. He was happy that someone had tried to understand him and his problems.

Understanding has to do with knowing and empathy has to do with feeling. Understanding and empathy can be and should be close allies. We need to take the time to understand and to empathize, to risk ourselves—and maybe a few quarters—to leave a positive impression upon the lives of others. We need more than just talk; we need to enter into people's lives and problems.

Listening

One lady responded to my survey, "At the end of a long day of homemaking, I need to talk to my husband. You know, he really listens. I love him." Another person said,

"He's always willing to hear what I have to say. I never have to feel that my small problems are unimportant."

Our culture seems to feel that talking is more important than listening. We respect and admire great orators, but who are the great listeners of our society? The question may seem silly, but nevertheless what the world needs is more listeners. Almost everyone I surveyed placed high value on a person who would listen.

We use four basic communication skills: reading, writing, speaking, and listening. You can take a course in any one of the first three, but seldom do you ever hear of a course on how to listen. If men would learn to listen to each other, many psychologists and psychiatrists would be out of work.

A friend told me about a counseling session he had with a woman who was having serious problems with her husband. The problem was so distressing that my friend felt unable to offer any meaningful help. After listening to her for nearly an hour, he apologized for being unable to offer a solution. Surprisingly, the lady responded, "You have helped me so much. I feel better now." He had helped her by simply giving her his full attention for a few important minutes.

Sociologist Tony Campolo in his book *Who Switched the Price Tags?* says that he gives his wife his complete attention when she speaks to him. "I hang on her every word and involve myself intensely in everything she is saying." Nothing pleases his wife more than when he listens intently and responsively.

Some people listen only for a break in the conversation so they can say what's on their mind. Often we miss the point of what someone is saying because we are so concerned with what we are going to say next. We read in Proverbs 18:13 that "he who answers before listening, this is his folly and his shame."

William Gladstone and Benjamin Disraeli, British statesmen, each served as prime minister during the long reign of Queen Victoria. Asked about her impressions of the two men, the queen said that when she was with Gladstone, "I feel I'm with one of the most important leaders in the world." About Disraeli she said, "He makes me feel as if I am one of the most important people in the world." She admired Gladstone, but admiration does not always lead to intimacy. The queen's comment about Disraeli was likely due to his interest in her as a person.

Good listeners have the concern and ability to ask good questions such as "How do you feel about that?" and "What do you think?" These kinds of questions show our interest in listening to a friend and open the way for more involvement with them.

During a convention at Notre Dame University in 1969, I had the opportunity to spend a few minutes alone with Supreme Court Chief Justice Earl Warren. The meeting is memorable not because he was an important public figure but because he gave me his full attention for those brief minutes. This gentle man listened to my questions completely and then gave me thoughtful answers. I have a lasting good memory of the meeting as a result.

Among the positive comments made about Thomas Foley when he became Speaker of the U.S. House of Representatives was, "You have his undivided attention regardless of who you are." These few words say a lot about his character and values.

For a number of reasons prevalent in our culture we fail to *hear* the feelings and needs of our acquaintances when they speak to us. And if they perceive that we are not truly hearing—at the feeling level—they will, of course, stop sharing.

Even our body language can tell others if we are listening or not. Looking around the room or at your watch instead of at the person communicates a lack of interest. Sadly, some men actually try to be detached and unavailable. Our gestures and eye movements are an important part of listening.

It has been my professional responsibility to teach students and to be sensitive to their needs. Sometimes following a long day, I'd come home planning to relax. If I was not careful—and sometimes I wasn't—I'd not listen well to my wife and children who needed my attention. I needed their attention too, and the best way to get attention is to be willing to give it.

Genuine listening is an act of recognition. In a sense it says, "You are important to me; I care about you and what you say." That's a major ingredient in friendship building.

Loyalty

These replies to the questionnaire pointed to the value of loyalty in a friend:

"When I tell Howard something in confidence, I know he will not spread it around town."

"He means what he says."

"If my close friend thinks I'm doing something self-destructive, he'll tell me."

Like a precious diamond, loyalty has many sparkling facets. For instance, the loyal friend is *not two-faced*. Gossip is cancerous to friendships. Immature people tend to gossip to gain attention. A loyal friend avoids these destructive conversations. A loyal friend will be honest with you, and he can be trusted not to betray you to others. A loyal friend knows that insincerity is likely to hinder a relationship.

In my study I have a picture of dozens of beautiful old redwood trees. The caption reads, "Quality endures."

Quality friendships endure the test of time mainly because of the loyalty of friends.

Commenting on his colleagues at Ford Motor Company, Lee Iacocca said that he was a hero until he was fired; then he was someone to be avoided at all costs. "I was hurting pretty bad after the firing. I could have used a phone call from somebody who said, 'Let's have coffee and feel terrific about what happened!' But most of my friends deserted me. It was the greatest shock of my life."[1]

People who responded to my questionnaire valued friends who do what they say they will do, who can be counted on to follow through with promises. The loyal friend *honors long-range commitments*, not easy in our fast-paced culture.

Friendship can be very fragile. Two New Jersey women, who had been friends for over fifteen years, wanted to try their luck at an Atlantic City casino. When they got to the slot machines, they decided to pool their money and divide equally any possible winnings. You guessed it! On that day one of the ladies hit a jackpot worth $327,296. But instead of sharing, the winner informed her friend that she intended to keep it all to herself.

This decision led to a court battle and, of course, an end to their friendship. The trial resulted in a division of the money between the two women. When the verdict was read, the friend who brought the lawsuit said, "I would rather have had our old friendship than the money."

In the 1970s' best-seller *Future Shock*, Alvin Toffler observes that ours is a throwaway society where even friendships are temporary. Commitments to friends, job, community, country, and even family are on the decline. The resulting lack of intimacy contributes to countless personal and social problems. Juvenile delinquency, divorce, mental illness, and child abuse are only a few examples.

The tragic irony is that many, in an effort to purge themselves of the unhappiness and loneliness caused by a lack of committed friends, actually want even more independence. We live in the so-called "me generation" where smart people "look out for number one." Some take assertiveness training, others demand their own rights. While this what's-in-it-for-me trend can help people with low self-images, overall it's destructive. If we neglect the needs of others, we all suffer.

Loyal friends are *flexible and tolerant of each other's idiosyncrasies*. Sometimes a great deal is required from one member of a friendship!

In his book *The Friendship Factor,* Alan Loy McGinnis describes a husband who had recently lost both his job and his self-confidence. He became difficult to live with and then impotent. His loyal wife, believing in her life-long commitment to her husband, knew he needed her now more than ever. McGinnis says there are periods in any relationship when one does most of the giving. It is a test of loyalty.

My wife has a friend from her high school days who was pretty and intelligent. She went on to college and graduate school and eventually received a master's degree in chemistry. Soon after she began her teaching career, she married a wonderful, handsome guy. One evening, some eight years later, she complained of a severe headache. Her husband took her to a nearby hospital, but the emergency room physician did not feel her condition was serious. It was not until the next day that it was discovered she had contracted spinal meningitis.

It's been nearly ten years since her husband learned that she would never be her normal self. She has difficulty reasoning or doing simple tasks. In many ways her behavior is childish. His dream of intellectual companionship and of a normal family life will never come true. Despite this, they are still together and he appears happy. He is not grudgingly meeting his responsibility—although there are bad days—rather he is living out the commitment he made to the woman he loves.

Most of us will not be called upon to show our loyalty to a friend or mate by having to make great sacrifices. Regardless of our situation, we need to look beyond our own needs. We need to stick by our friends. This may seem strange to the what's-in-it-for-me crowd, but with the help of God, this is how we give and receive happiness.

Self-Disclosure

On every questionnaire, respondents said that those closest to them are people willing to disclose their feelings and needs.

"John called on me when he needed help. I didn't feel imposed upon; in fact, I felt privileged he turned to me."

"Becky lets me know what her own needs are."

"Marty doesn't try to pretend she doesn't have problems too."

"I feel a part of his life."

We often fail to open ourselves to others out of fear of rejection. If you open up, you take a risk. You become vulnerable. Since dependency is often interpreted as weakness, men tend to fear sharing their emotions with others.

Of course, you shouldn't disclose your needs to those who are not interested or when it's obviously inappropriate. But as a relationship develops, individuals naturally share needs, problems, expectations, fears, wants, and even weaknesses. If you hide your feelings or present an unreal front, you may be viewed as unapproachable. Then friendships remain superficial.

Don't be afraid to ask for help. No one wants to be a pest, but too often the I-don't-want-to-be-a-burden argument is a smokescreen we use to avoid a closer relationship. An extreme example of how far some will go before they reach out to others occurred in 1989. A former Pennsylvania minister, unemployed and too proud to accept handouts, brought tragedy to his family. He rejected welfare and refused to send his children to a public school where they would have qualified for free lunch programs. His fourteen-year-old son died from starvation, and his wife and other children were hospitalized for malnutrition.

Strange as it may seem at first, people feel warm toward those who are willing to receive. We believe it is more blessed to give than to receive. (See Acts 20:35.) While this injunction is true, it doesn't mean we shouldn't receive. *Too many of us are stingy receivers.* Jesus often began a new relationship by asking for food, lodging, or fellowship; we tend to withdraw from people who seem to be self-sufficient. With his willingness to receive, Christ gave others an opportunity to give. We like to help. We want to be useful. Talk to virtually any elderly American, and you will hear some comment about wanting to be useful. We do no one a favor by removing opportunities for them to contribute to the lives of others.

A friend I liked a great deal was older than I and had accumulated a good deal of wisdom. He was kind and willing to share with me, and I was grateful for his positive influence. After a time, however, I felt somewhat uneasy. I think I now know what the problem was. I was always on the receiving end of the friendship. My friend conveyed the impression that he didn't have any needs. At best it was a lopsided relationship like that of the Lone Ranger and Tonto. My friend wore an emotional mask that prevented me from ever doing any giving in the relationship.

When a person feels needed, he feels important. A school administrator could not understand why the teachers in his district were grumbling and generally suffering from low morale. After all, why should they complain? They were among the best-paid faculty in all the state. But they did not feel needed or important. When collective bargaining was introduced in the school system, an adversary relationship was established. Teachers, while well paid, were no longer recognized for a job well done.

We never outgrow our need to be a necessary member of some group. We need to feel important. We need to be told we're doing a good job. Many psychologists feel that a major reason retirement is such a difficult adjustment for most men is that they no longer have the sense of being needed.

In addition to the fear of rejection, we tend to hold people at arm's length because we want to be admired. Robert Mitchum talks about his late friend John Wayne. He says the Duke was six feet four inches tall but still wore four-inch shoe lifts and a ten gallon hat. Mitchum says that Wayne once confided, "You gotta keep them Wayne-conscious." It's difficult to be yourself and be honest in relationships when you have a desire to be admired.

If people knew our true selves, without our social masks, they wouldn't admire us—or so our reasoning goes. It's unfortunate that we are not more transparent. The emotionally secure individual expects to like and trust others. He also expects to be liked by others and is therefore less likely to feel a need to hide.

Openness produces openness. Proverbs advises that to have friends, we need to be friendly (17:17; 18:24; 27:6; 27:10). Friendships must be reciprocal.

Compromise

"I'm glad Bob doesn't always insist on getting his own way."

"Bill is willing to consider what I think."

Some men think being firm and unaltering in their decisions is a sign of strength. But how can it be weakness to be sensitive to others?

Psychologist Clyde Narramore believes that one sign of the mentally healthy person is being neither a dictator nor a doormat. Narramore encourages us both to have and to express convictions, but not to the extent that we disregard the convictions and feelings of others.

An unwillingness to compromise is actually a manifestation of immaturity. A young woman said, "When I was dating, I liked being told what to do. Now I've grown up and I don't like men who are rigid and insensitive to my ideas."

Friends compromise on matters of personal convenience, not on matters of personal values or principles. Sam Rayburn, Speaker of the U.S. House of Representatives during the fifties, once said that "any jackass can kick a barn down, but it takes a carpenter to build one." The Congress must learn compromise if there is to be progress in the nation's business. So must friends.

A dictionary defines *compromise* as "a settlement of differences in which each side makes concessions." A suburban housewife in Chicago said that if her husband, just once in a while, would take her to a concert or out to dinner, she wouldn't mind spending two weeks each summer with him on a fishing trip to northern Wisconsin. If we compromise, others compromise, allowing friendships to develop.

We look for these six qualities of friendship in others if we truly want to develop intimate emotional relationships. Now for the hard question: Do you have these traits within yourself? Demonstrating them in your own life will open the door for genuine friendships.

DISCUSSION QUESTIONS

1. Which qualities of friendship listed in this chapter do you and the important people in your life possess?
2. Discuss the meaning of this statement: "Friends compromise on matters of personal convenience, not on matters of personal principles."
3. In what ways is listening an important communication skill in the making and keeping of friendships?
4. Having read Chapters 6 and 7, you are probably aware of the indirect relationships between biblical principles and positive friendship qualities. They correlate very well. Use the following chart for discussion of their relationship.

Friendship qualities we look for in others	*Biblical principles of friendship*
empathy	God-centered values
acceptance	covenant formation
listening	respect
loyalty	faithfulness
self-disclosure	candor
compromise	involvement

CHAPTER EIGHT

The Stages of Friendship

Be slow to fall into friendship; but when thou art in, continue firm and constant.

—Socrates

We are admonished to love everyone, but must we love all individuals with the same intensity and involvement? Of course you can't do it, but should your love be somehow divided equally among the people you know? And should you feel guilty because you have failed to live up to those democratic expectations? Each of these questions deserves a definite answer of *no*. Scripture requires that we love others, to be sure, but this love is bound to take different forms and be expressed in many different ways. Biblical principles of love and friendship are just that—principles. Like all principles they should be applied differently, depending on how well you know and how deeply you care for another man.

Jesus formed friendships easily with men and women as well as with children. People with different social positions and views of the world were drawn to him. Many were aware of his love and concern for them as individuals. But despite his agape love for each and every person, he related to people differently. **103**

Many are surprised to learn that the Lord did not treat everyone the same. From his large group of followers and disciples, Christ felt the need to select a small group of twelve men to work and fellowship with more intimately. This important and assumingly difficult selection process was preceded by a night of prayer.

Who were the men Jesus picked to work closely with him? The apostles were a diverse group of human beings. They were not the men we have stereotyped and immortalized in stained glass. The almost effeminate and saintly mental images many harbor do not represent the men who were closest to the Savior. Their personalities contained flaws as well as virtues. Most were very young fishermen who labored with their hands. They had little education and no training in theology. Only three left a written account of their days with Jesus; the remaining nine were probably illiterate. In the entire group, there was not a priest or a single member of the upper class. These, then, were ordinary, common men who usually failed to understand Jesus' teachings and occasionally even undermined his efforts because of personal ambitions.

Jesus developed friendships with non-perfect people, providing us an important example. We're rather foolish and ethnocentric if we expect perfection from our friends. Jesus selected imperfect men not just to advance the kingdom of God but *because, in his humanness, he too needed fellowship*. The large crowds that followed him around Galilee could not satisfy the need for close friendship.

Christ developed closer relationships with the apostles than he did with other devoted followers. And within the group of twelve were three who shared even closer companionship with him. Jesus developed a deeper stage of friendship with Peter, James, and John than he did with the others. Even among the three, Jesus was closer to the apostle John than to Peter or James.

The biographical account of Christ's life provides evidence that it is not only undesirable, it's impossible to treat everyone in the same fashion. Experts estimate that each of us has a pool of from 500 to 2,500 acquaintances. Each of us confides in and feels closer to some individuals more than others. This is quite natural since we have neither the emotional capacity nor the time to share intimately with everyone. And not everyone we know has the emotional energy, time, or desire to be very close to us. If we are sensitive to this latter fact, it will help us overcome feelings of being neglected by other men.

Some men develop close friends rapidly. Jonathan and David are one example. Others develop closeness over a longer period of time, like Peter and Paul. And still others, like Job and Eliphaz, never manage to become close friends. While the time required to cultivate a friendship may vary, all friendships go through specific stages. And in each stage our words, thoughts, and actions are different. Where we are in a relationship affects how we behave.

There are at least three distinct stages or levels of interpersonal relationships. For convenience we will refer to these levels as *acquaintance, companionship, and established friendship.* This chapter will examine each stage and suggest ways to maintain a close friendship.

Stage 1: Acquaintance

An acquaintance can be a stranger at a party, an interesting person we meet on an airplane, or a next-door neighbor we may have known for several years. The length of time we know an individual is not important in an acquaintance relationship. Many of us have worked for years with individuals we do not know well or feel close to emotionally. These people are and probably will remain mere acquaintances.

Conversation with acquaintances is sporadic and rarely goes beyond safe topics. These could include shop talk, the best fertilizer to use on the lawn, the weather, or one's golf game. Safe topics have low emotional content and allow us to talk while, at the same time, keeping under wraps our beliefs and feelings. Subjects with high emotional content are inappropriate conversation topics at this level.

A relationship at the acquaintance stage is likely to be based on where we live or work rather than on common values or goals. If we move, change jobs, or shop in a different part of town, we drop our casual acquaintance relationships in the old neighborhood, at our previous jobs, or at the previous stores. Most of these relationships form because of what sociologists refer to as *propinquity*, or physical nearness. They quickly disintegrate if we remove ourselves from day-to-day contact with the people. No other reason exists to maintain the relationship.

In many circumstances it is advantageous to maintain impersonal relationships. For example, business, legal, educational, and military interpersonal contacts are frequently formalized and impersonal. Max Weber, the nineteenth-century German sociologist, in his classic studies of bureaucracy, recognized the wisdom of formalizing certain kinds of human interaction in order to maintain objectivity, impartiality, and equality of treatment. Theoretically, favoritism is not an issue in bureaucratic decision-making. Promotions are based on ability rather than friendship or nepotism.

But impersonality within corporate America is often

carried to extremes. Men who are merely acquaintances could at least exchange a brief pleasantry on occasion. Men need to shed the stern face and learn to smile more often. One need not be a close companion to extend courtesies to contacts during a normal day.

A friend of mine, Dr. Jay Thompson of Ball State University, is working with foremen in factories to improve communication and reduce conflict between workmen at different levels of responsibility. The foremen are encouraged to apply simple psychological principles in working with the men and women on the assembly line. Such common niceties as greeting workers with a "hello" or "how's it going" are truly appreciated. The foremen also are encouraged to praise good workmanship and to use positive rather than negative reinforcement. In short, Dr. Thompson encourages these men and women to "be nice" to the people they work with. The result is a more pleasant working relationship for everyone.

There is a footnote to this story. One of the foremen told Dr. Thompson, "You know, my wife and I are getting along better lately." Courtesy, kindness, and thoughtfulness are principles that apply to all human relationships, regardless of the depth of personal commitment.

A 1989 Johns Hopkins School of Public Health study revealed that employees who are allowed to talk to workers during the day have more healthy hearts. Employees with little freedom to talk to others on the job have higher rates of heart disease. Apparently, small talk with coworkers around the water cooler is good for your health.

Put people at ease in your presence. The writer of Hebrews tells us "to show hospitality to strangers" (Heb. 13:2 RSV).

A starting point can be a smile, a greeting, a kind word, or an interested question. Phrase your questions in terms of the other person's interests. Every person has an interesting story to tell if given the opportunity.

The very least we can do at this stage is to make a conscious effort to learn the name of our new acquaintance. Be pleasant; ask questions that reveal both interest and acceptance; listen well to what he says. When you meet a second time, use his name—he'll appreciate the fact that you thought enough of him to at least remember his name. And using the name also helps you remember it. But if you don't remember his name, don't try to fake it. Say, "I'm sorry. Tell me your name again."

The key to an enjoyable, long-standing acquaintance relationship, such as with a fellow employee at work, is to be pleasant and simply treat the other person in the fashion you would expect to be treated—the Golden Rule approach. The poet Wordsworth wrote in his piece "Lines Composed a Few Miles Above Tintern Abbey": "That best portion of a good man's life, / His little, nameless, unremembered acts / Of kindness and of love." Most acts of kindness are remembered by those who receive them.

Herb Goldberg, in his widely read book *The Hazards of Being Male*, argues that it is extremely difficult for a man to progress beyond the first, superficial stage of interpersonal relationships. Goldberg attributes this inability to early negative conditioning. "By college days all men have already been thoroughly contaminated by the competitive posture which undermines the possibility of genuine intimacy."[1] Male relationships therefore, according to Goldberg, begin and remain at a manipulative level.

Following ten years of research, Daniel Levinson, commenting about the topic of male friendship, said, "In our interviews, friendship was largely noticeable by its absence. Close friendship with a man or a woman is rarely experienced by American men."[2] These are strong and pessimistic conclusions expressed by both Goldberg and Levinson; however, other social scientists also feel that male relationships are usually superficial and self-serving.

Joseph Bensman and Robert Zilienfeld conclude from their research that young individuals "work to create friendships outside the family in an effort to create a self independent of the family, and to develop defenses against family invasions of an autonomous self."[3] But while the relationships of many men remain at a shallow level, those who understand and apply biblical principles of friendship can develop deeper, more meaningful relationships.

An acquaintance relationship, while lacking in emotional attachment, need not be self-serving or manipulative. On the other hand, relationships do remain shallow if the parties are interested only in them for self-serving reasons. Men may progress to higher levels of relationship if they know and apply biblical principles of friendship. A proverb says that "a few close friends are more valuable than a host of acquaintances." This is true, but it's also true that all close friendships were at one time mere acquaintances. Don't underestimate your opportunity to find companions or friends from people who are now only acquaintances. But don't wait. Get started today.

Author Tom Powers says, "We speak, when we speak at all, of neutral things and take a long time to be at ease with each other, and let years go by just as if we had five lifetimes in which to be friends and could afford to squander this one."[4]

Stage 2: Companionship

If acquaintances hit it off—are able to communicate and share something in common—they form what may be

termed a *companionship*. Sharing something in common
is a vital ingredient to a companionship. At this stage men
share common goals rather than common core values.
Men join teams, flirt with women, and go off to war together. Their togetherness is often based on a task to be
performed or a goal to be obtained. Goldberg says that
men can come comfortably close to each other only when
they are sharing a common target. While *target* is a word
too narrow and too negative in connotation, it nevertheless is often appropriate.

Researchers Shils and Janowitz, in 1948, conducted a
study of the cohesion and disintegration of the Nazi army.
Although outnumbered and being beaten badly, the German soldiers fought on with great effectiveness. Many
attributed their tenacity to their strong political convictions. The study revealed, however, that the commitment to continue fighting was related to membership in a
squad. As long as the squad members both gave and received affection within the group, they were prepared to
fight regardless of their individual political attitudes. Being buddies or companions sustained them because of
common goals or a feeling of belonging rather than common values.

American men are certainly group oriented. We're big
on joining groups. Men invented the voluntary association
with such early forms as freemasonry. Recent examples of
popular voluntary male associations are fraternal and service organizations, country clubs, weekly poker parties,
and youth gangs, which in the early nineties are nearly
taking over some inner cities.

Unlike acquaintances, companions schedule time together. They go beyond the "Hi, how are you?" syndrome
that's associated with happenstance meetings. Buddies
enjoy each other's company, and although the relationship may exist for many years, usually it is based largely

on the immediate satisfactions that come with companionship.

Two lawyers I know have played golf together on a regular basis for many years. They enjoy the togetherness of playing a game, but they make few comments that are not related to the game of golf. They truly do not know each other but are able nevertheless to enjoy the satisfaction that comes from companionship. Unlike women, men are more able—or perhaps I should say more willing—to relate to segments or aspects of another's personality. Women, in contrast, assume a holistic approach to human personality.

This companionship level of relationship, while satisfying and even intense at times, will not stand up well to emotional stress or individual conflicts regarding values or interests. There is little commitment in a companionship, as each man knows that if a real problem occurs, he cannot or will not turn to the companion for assistance. Men do not seek out a buddy when they need help in time of a personal crisis. This is especially true for men of marginal economic status, as William Whyte and Elliot Liebow have researched and eloquently written about in the classic studies *Street Corner Society* and *Talley's Corner.*

Recently, one of the golfing attorneys was quite ill and required emergency surgery. For several days he was in rather serious condition. At their next golf outing, the companion said to the fully recovered man, "I hear you were quite ill. Is everything okay now?" The fortunate man responded, "I'm just fine. In fact, I'm so good, I'll beat the pants off you on the course today."

They both laughed and that was it. Nothing else was said about the illness. It's strange somehow that the man when sick had made no effort to communicate with his companion. And the companion, when hearing of the illness through the clubhouse grapevine, made no effort to contact his buddy. Then with the interruption behind them, both were willing to return to their regular weekly round of golf.

Despite the lack of a long-range commitment, companionships serve the important functions of providing fellowship. They give the warm feeling of belonging, similar to the three musketeers credo—all for one and one for all.

When asked why he returned to coaching football, Bud Wilkinson said, "The emotional aspects of the game are stronger than anywhere else. The feelings you had toward shipmates in World War II, those are the feelings you have in athletics." Many players today have a difficult time adjusting to their post-playing years without the companions on the team. Companions give a man a feeling of confidence about his value as a man.

The two most serious problems in achieving and maintaining a companionship are trust and dominance, according to Goldberg's research. He suggests that we as men must understand the kinds of behavior that could destroy the confidence we have in each other. To handle the issue of dominance, each man should consciously work toward equalizing power and decision-making so that neither ends up in the shadow of the other. For example, men might arrange tagalong sessions at work or recreation where each man is able to display his strengths and interests.

Companionship may not be friendship, but it is a type of relationship we need. You can deepen a relationship by making an effort to learn more about the men you know as companions. It isn't inappropriate to ask probing questions that are thoughtful and other-person centered. Be trustworthy and dependable, but don't try to appear perfect or all-powerful. If your friend wants to share a problem, listen well. Companionships need nourishment, for they, like other levels of interpersonal relationships, can be fragile.

Men have frail egos and rarely work at a friendship. We turn off with the slightest provocation and hide our true selves from others. Few acquaintances or companionships therefore evolve into actual friendships. While true friendships may be a rarity, they can be developed if we are willing to invest the necessary time and emotional energy.

Stage 3: Established Friendship

Some men seek to fulfill needs that companionship alone cannot satisfy. Companions who share basic similar values and who invest the necessary time and attention can establish friendships. And when a close friendship is established, it can slip away from you if it is taken for granted or in other ways neglected. Only quality relationships endure.

In Chapter 6, we surveyed biblical principles of friendship at some length. In this section we will consider the maintenance of established friendships.

"I know that the dissolution of a personal friendship is among the most painful occurrences in human life." So wrote President Jefferson to James Monroe. The ancient Roman Seneca said, "To lose a friend is the greatest of evils."

In a *Psychology Today* magazine study, people were asked to indicate what factors led to a friendship's cooling off or ending. Among the most frequently checked reasons, in the most frequently mentioned order, were:

1. One of us moved.
2. I felt that my friend betrayed me.

3. We discovered that we had very different views on issues that are important to me.
4. One of us got married.
5. My friend became involved with (or married) someone I didn't like.
6. A friend borrowed money from me.
7. We took a vacation together.
8. One of us had a child.
9. One of us became markedly more successful at work.
10. I got divorced.
11. My friend got divorced.
12. One of us became much richer.
13. I borrowed money from a friend.[5]

These responses, while interesting, do not reveal the symptoms of a dying friendship, but rather seem to indicate a sudden breaking off of the relationship. C. S. Lewis noted that people do not suddenly renounce their faith in God due to some event or newly acquired insight. Rather, over a long period of neglect, the once strong relationship between man and God slowly dies. I believe this same process of neglect describes how a friendship between men dies.

Friendships require the continual application of biblical principles with special attention in certain areas. The maintenance of a friendship requires that we not lose sight of three underlying factors:

- Commit yourself to your friend.
- Resist judgmental attitudes.
- Accept the love of your friend.

After you develop a close friendship with its inherent intimacy, these factors become especially important. Let's consider each one.

Close friends must consciously establish and renew commitment. Commitments are not popular today. They imply inconvenience. We are bombarded with a self-indulgent, hedonistic ethic that centers on self rather than the other. This aspect of our culture works to undermine our friendships. Commitment is not popular and it may be a burden, but it is essential to the care and feeding of a friendship.

At a shopping center, I saw a girl wearing a T-shirt that read "If it feels good do it." It's difficult for me to understand how a young woman could display such a phrase without embarrassment, even if she were unaware of its suggestive connotation. This phrase illustrates the value system of our age. It implies that "I'll do whatever pleases me, and if my pleasure gets in your way—too bad for you." This self-centered value system is the antithesis of the commitment needed to sustain friendship.

Commitment develops slowly and logically. "Commitment is not irrational. It would be foolish to trust a foothold you had not properly tested or to marry a person you have not adequately assessed or to trust a message you have not investigated. But commitment requires more than reason. It requires the act of faith. Then the sense of risk fades and hope grows."[6]

Misfortune is often a test of commitment. When friends come to our aid or defense in time of need, the relationship between us grows more secure and satisfying. We tend to reveal our true colors during times of stress. This truth is illustrated in one of Aesop's Fables, "Two Travelers and a Bear":

> Two men were traveling in company through a forest, when, all at once, a huge bear crashed out of the brush near them.
>
> One of the men, thinking of his own safety, climbed a tree.

The other, unable to fight the savage beast alone, threw himself on the ground and lay still, as if he were dead. He had heard that a bear will not touch a dead body.

It must have been true for the bear snuffed at the man's head awhile, and then, seeming to be satisfied that he was dead, walked away.

The man in the tree climbed down.

"It looked as if that bear whispered something in your ear," he said. "What did he tell you?"

"He said," answered the other, "that it was not at all wise to keep company with a fellow who would desert his friend in a moment of danger."

Women retain more friends than men because, while male friends share activities, women who are friends exchange confidences. Why? Perhaps because men may be more aware of the risk of being judged when they confide in friends. I remember painfully a friend who shared with me in confidence. I was involved in his life and concerned about his well-being. Knowing this he took a risk and became vulnerable. However, I reacted too strongly to the problem he confided to me and nearly lost a friend.

The problem was infidelity. When he approached me, he no longer was engaged in the adulterous relationship; he was then trying to work through his feelings of guilt. He had asked God to forgive his sin but somehow the memory just wouldn't go away. He opened up to me, wanting counsel and acceptance. Unfortunately, I did not follow the Bible's directive for this type of situation. "Brethren, if a man is overtaken in any trespass, you who are spiritual restore such a one in a spirit of gentleness" (Gal. 6:1). Gentle? Not me. Supercilious is a more accurate description of my behavior.

I hardly heard a word he said. It never entered my mind that it must have been difficult for him to share this sin with me. I was too busy moralizing to see his pain. I exerted little effort trying to understand how he got himself into this predicament. Being judgmental I responded emotionally instead of reasonably. I failed. Listening and showing honest Christian love would not have minimized the sin, but it might have helped a friend. Friends must resist being judgmental.

Close friends have love for each other. In one study a full 92 percent believed that friendship is a form of love. The greatest comment on love in all the Bible, and perhaps in all literature, is recorded in 1 Corinthians 13:4–8. Read this brief section of Scripture, and apply its principles to a friendship.

Close friends provide support during trials as well as during accomplishments. Friends even help each other to accomplish life goals. Close friends don't ignore character flaws but offer, request, and accept concern and assistance in the correction of possible personality problems.

It seems a paradox, but friends also respect each other's individuality and independence. While remaining available, friends do not become careless with the other's need to be alone, either physically or mentally. A close friend knows the real you, and loves you anyway. But you should be open to accept expressions of his concern and encouragement.

In earlier chapters we saw that people, regardless of gender, need emotionally supportive relationships. We all have emotional needs which if unmet leave us unhappy or physically or mentally ill. And yet many of us resist these relationships. This may well be our biggest problem—the unwillingness to let other people love us, truly love us. We would rather "tough it out" or "grit our teeth" or "take it like a man." Many men, even those who apply biblical principles, tend to go it alone when they have problems.

Perhaps we have a latent fear of being accused of being too close to another man and therefore suspected of being homosexual. More likely, however, we as men have simply been raised to believe the myth that masculinity and independence are synonymous. And we are often too proud to seek help or accept demonstrations of love. And we know that if we accept love, later we may feel obligated to return love when it may be inconvenient. So instead of receiving or giving, we clam up and withhold—and in the process, lose out.

Within each man is a dark castle with a fierce dragon to guard the gate. Living in this castle is a lonely self, a self most men have suppressed, a self they are afraid to show. He's protected by an armored knight who keeps outsiders at sword's length, even those who manage to slip by the dragon and sneak into the castle.

When men take a risk—cage the dragon, give the knight some time off, and lower the drawbridge—and let down the barriers, they begin to respond to others as whole persons and try to communicate with openness and intimacy. Their openness brings opportunity for a growing relationship, for a wider range of deeply felt experiences. And this is the stuff from which friendships are formulated and sustained.

DISCUSSION QUESTIONS

1. Human flaws become evident when two men become friends. Discuss whether you accept the limitations of others or expect perfection. Remember, Jesus established friendships with imperfect people.
2. Christ had friendships with people of different backgrounds and personalities. Is this true for you? Should it be?

3. How do you explain the seemingly contradictory feelings of fear and the desire for closeness? Does intimacy scare you? Why or why not?
4. How should you respond when a friend confides in you that he has sinned? Refer to Galatians 6:1 as you consider this question.

Friendship in Other Times and Places

A friend is one to whom one may pour out all the contents of one's heart, chaff and grain together, knowing that the gentlest of hands will take and sift it, keep what is worth keeping, and with a breath of kindness, blow the rest away.

—Arabian proverb

Is friendship the same wherever you go? Do people understand friendship to mean something specific, or does the word have very different meanings depending on one's culture or one's period in history?

We know that the family as a social institution exists in all societies. Even revolutionary societies have failed when they tried to alter or eliminate family structure. The family is one of God's creation ordinances and exists in every culture, in every country.

But what about friendship?

Friendship is ubiquitous in history and culture. It is integral to the psychological, social, and spiritual health of individuals and societies as is the family. Friendship, like marriage and family, is a gift to us from the Lord. It is for us to protect, nurture, and enjoy.

We often let nationalistic, social, and cultural differences cloud the reality that we are but one human race created by a loving God. Acts 17:26 tells us

120

that "from one man he made every nation of men" (NIV). Our feelings and our needs are universal.

Dr. Robert Brain, an anthropologist, studied several tribes which are, on the surface, much different from our Western culture. Yet, people in every one of these tribes manifested a need to reach out to others, a need to make social contact and to form friendships. The similarity of humanity is equally evident from a sample reading of authors throughout history—Aristotle, Plato, Cicero, Homer, Montaigne, Pascal, and C. S. Lewis. Letters or diaries of average people written generations ago reveal the same feelings and needs we experience today.

Friendship Across the World

Dr. Cora DuBois and several other social scientists have concluded the following from extended cross-cultural research:

- *Friendship is a universal phenomenon.* Not every person has the emotional capacity or the social opportunity to develop a friendship, but friendship as a relationship occurs in all societies.
- *Friendship is affected by many factors* including marriage, sexuality, kinship system, and superordinate-subordinate relationships.
- *Friendships are voluntary* in that they are not imposed by the culture or ascribed at birth.
- *Friendships are reciprocal.* The action of giving and taking flows both ways.
- *Friendships are dyadic.* The most widely valued type of friendship is between two people, although the interpersonal relationship between members of gangs, teams, or clubs has characteristics associated with friendship.

Friendships exist between two people. History records effort after effort to establish communes or utopias on the basis of intimate fellowship. Thirty years ago, in the 1960s, we witnessed a resurgent attempt to establish friendship communities or communes. These are almost always doomed to failure. It is hard enough to sustain a dyadic or two-person friendship. To sustain a complex, multiple friendship is nearly impossible.

Therefore, friendship is a personal relationship. In America, friendship is also private, which is a rare phenomenon. The friendship can be established and maintained independent of the different social groups the friends belong to. In other words, the relationship is socially autonomous.

- *Friendships are characterized by confidence, trust, and intimacy.* The bonding relationship of friendship is an important characteristic of all human cultures.

Assuredly, the behavior associated with friendship varies immensely as one travels from culture to culture. But this fact notwithstanding, an underlying similarity of beliefs and values about friendship can be discovered in many areas of the world and at different times in the world's history.

The *Encyclopedia of Social Sciences* summarizes basic values of friendships that exist in most cultures. Friendship includes closeness, solidarity, absence of ulterior ends, reciprocity, and a playing down of social distinctions such as age, sex, and social class. Friendship obligations and rights are secondary to other, usually family, responsibilities. And yet friendship is intimate, important, and enduring. Friendship is associated by rites of passage or ceremonial entry. Friendship involves the exchanging of gifts and/or economic support.

In most cultures, friendship involves voluntary commitment, intimacy, and spontaneity, and is valued by the society as a source for personal growth and security. Perhaps this is why being friendless often involves personal feelings of shame.

Despite differences in customs, every known culture places important emphasis upon the love and loyalty between friends. Anthropologist Robert Brain says that *"affection and loyalty are implicit in all friendships in all societies."* Undivided loyalty and altruistic love are valued highly throughout the world, but this shouldn't be any great surprise. After all, people are far more similar than they are different.

Cultural Universals

In an important book, *The Proper Study of Mankind*, author Steward Chase cataloged thirty-three cultural universals of humankind. A cultural universal is an aspect of human behavior that is demonstrated in almost every culture on the planet. Think of it. Despite the tremendous apparent outward diversity of behavior among the hundreds, perhaps thousands, of different cultures within the world's approximately 170 nations, we have much in common. Following is a sample of these universal culture traits:

1. A form of religion and ethics prevail.
2. There is an established government and laws.
3. There is a permanent family structure; monogamy is the usual form of marriage.
4. The family cares for the aged as well as the young.
5. Divorce is recognized but not approved.
6. Society provides punishment for infringements of its rules.
7. The male is the formal ruler of the family and of society.

8. Free giving is a high virtue.
9. There is a sense of loyalty to the nation or tribe.
10. None of the societies has complete communal ownership of property.
11. Friends are limited to the same sex.

Friendship is one of Chase's universal cultural traits. In most cultures a man feels a sense of shame if he lacks an intimate friendship. Aristotle reflected this feeling when he said that "Without friends no one would choose to live." But this universal belief in friendship's importance has another aspect.

Perhaps you're surprised by statement number 11. Probably no greater restriction exists upon friendship than that it must be limited to individuals of the same sex. Both cross-cultural and historical information show that in nearly every culture on earth, both present and past, cross-sex friendships have not been cultivated.

The common belief is that men and women can be lovers but never friends. There is evidence that men attempt to develop cross-sex friendships as a means of sexual exploitation. Sociologist Robert Bell found that in cross-sex friendships, the men were usually older and better educated and usually wanted the relationship to end up in the bedroom. A high degree of sexuality was either implied or expressed in cross-sex friendships. Furthermore, these cross-sex relationships were usually superficial and ritualistic.[1]

In a survey conducted by *Psychology Today*, three-fourths of the respondents believed that cross-sex platonic friendships were complicated due to sexual tensions, the lack of encouragement by society, and the fact that man/woman members of a relationship have less in common than friends of the same sex.

If either member of a cross-sex friendship is married,

respondents felt that something must be wrong or missing from that marriage. Why else would someone of the opposite sex other than the spouse be needed for intimate emotional involvement? A spouse is bound to feel threatened by a close cross-sex friendship, partially due to the potential for physical intimacy.

It is true in a few cultures where women are highly valued, and daily accessibility to members of the opposite sex exists in different areas of life, and where cross-sex platonic friendship is culturally encouraged that a cross-sex friendship can exist, remain nonsexual, and provide emotional satisfaction. The Bangwa of Africa have strong male-female friendships that are never confused with love affairs. But the Bangwa culture type is extremely rare. Where cross-sex friendships exist at all, they tend to be limited to young, unmarried people. Sociologist Bell has found few references to socially approved close friendships between men and women that had no courtship or sexual implications.

We need not be strictly homo-social, but the fact remains that in American society our social lives are based on pair relationships, either as marriage partners or as same-sex friends.

Rather than attempt to seek emotional gratification from women other than their own wives, men need to place more value on their emotional ties with men.

It seems, from a review of societies existing prior to our own age, that men and women came together either when it was time to eat or time to go to bed. Throughout American history the major taboos against cross-sex friendship have been based on the belief that women were less capable of friendship than men. For example, philosopher George Santayana wrote that "Friendship with a woman is therefore apt to be more or less than friendship; less, because there is no intellectual parity; more, because (even when the relation remains wholly dispassionate, as in respect to old ladies) there is something mysterious and oracular about a woman's mind which inspires a certain instinctive deference and puts it out of the question to judge what she says by male standards."[2]

Christ did not ignore women. On the contrary, during a time when women suffered extreme discrimination, Jesus treated women with respect and dignity. "Godly women were influential in Jesus' background, i.e., Elizabeth, Mary, Anna, the sinner of Luke 7:36–40, Mary Magdalene, Martha and Mary of Bethany, and the women at the empty tomb. But Christ formulated His most intimate friendships with men, Peter, James and John for example."[3]

Privacy or Community

Americans tend to be lonely. Our culture was founded partially on the Christian love of God and love of neighbor. But even with this basis, or in spite of it, we are some of the loneliest people on earth.

In most societies people do not experience loneliness, at least to the nagging, acute degree that Americans do. In other cultures people are rarely alone either physically or emotionally. Relatives, neighbors, and even strangers are a normal part of everyone's life.

Not so in America. Our emphasis on privacy has been deadly to our emotional well-being. I know a school principal who divorced his wife two years ago after his children were grown. Now he has few responsibilities beyond the end of the work day. He lives in an urban community at some distance from his school district, and he has no commitment to his neighborhood. "I have nothing to live up to," he told me, "and no one to please after 4:30 in the afternoon. I can do as I please with my time, my money, and my relationships."

In most cultures the image of a private, independent life denotes sadness. But in America we tend to envy the freedom that comes with the private life. Bachelors, like the principal, are frequently seen as carefree, when in reality they are often lonely and more likely to die at an earlier age than married men.

Unlike any other culture, our acute loneliness must be seriously considered in the search for solutions to nagging contemporary societal problems. Loneliness and a lack of commitment to others are factors in our high suicide, divorce, alcoholism, drug, murder, rape, and abortion rates.

Anthropologist Robert Brain mentions that even the most reserved people, because of loneliness, now look for companionship through special groups such as Parents Without Partners, in singles bars, in gay bars, at cocktail parties, and through computer dating services. These groups tend to manufacture false situations. One puts on a plastic smile and is generous with his affection, but only for the moment.

The artificial ambiance of forced jollity fosters the pathetic hope that a "meaningful relationship" may evolve. But as long as we ignore God's principles for developing a relationship, it of course never will.

People from other cultural backgrounds find it difficult to understand why we cherish personal freedom to such an extreme degree. To them, personal independence, to the extent we seek it, is viewed as a form of isolation or of being ostracized. With the songwriter of "Me and Bobby McGee," they might agree that "freedom's just another word for nothing left to lose."

Many Western nations including the United States have sacrificed emotional intimacy on the false altar of personal freedom. Many American males have never experienced a close male friendship or known what it means to care for a male friend. Those who do have friends usually have experienced low levels of trust and personal sharing and generally invest little in these relationships. The very few who have established intimate male friendships have done so with at least a degree of guilt and peer ridicule.

The parable of the rich fool (Luke 12:16–20) has several appropriate applications for us today. The man, for example, was a fool because of his inordinate emphasis on materialism at the expense of developing intimacy with others; his belief that his belongings were his own and were the measure of self-worth and importance; his preoccupation with storing instead of sharing; and his idea that he could feed his soul with bread. This lifestyle does not fit God's order. That's why Jesus called the man a fool.

The rich fool, however, would feel more at home in mainstream America than in many other cultures that are less materialistic and more caring. For example, he would feel out of place if he were living with the Zuni Indians of New Mexico where cooperation is more the economic norm. With the Zuni, and in countless other cultures, the respected people are cooperative, friendly, and generous with time and possessions. They are not concerned with accumulating more goods or property than they can use, and if they do acquire wealth, they are expected to share it. In contrast with the rich fool of Luke 12, the Zuni have a common storehouse for agricultural surplus to be shared by all. Emphasis is devoted to developing relationships, not to competition and the accumulation of wealth.

But to American men the term *friend* is lacking in content. It is devoid of emotion and commitment. We rarely know what someone means when he declares, "He is my friend." After all, many of us have used the word to refer to someone who seems to be a pleasant fellow since first meeting him some thirty minutes earlier.

Unlike several other cultures, the American society is less structured and formal in its social relationships. This social climate, which encourages spontaneity, has drawbacks as well as advantages. Our relationships are usually shallow, one-dimensional, unfulfilling, and often short-lived. We have few assurances that our current friends will still be our friends a few months down the road.

In other cultures, friendship, like marriage or parenting, is binding. In some areas of the world, friendship is elevated to a status equal to marriage and encompassed with ceremony and ritual. The concept of blood brotherhood, for example, is found in many societies.

It is not imperative for friendship to be established with ritual and sustained by specific societal requirements, but anthropologists have found that in most cultures of the past and present, love between friends has not been allowed to depend on the vague bonds of mere emotional sentiment. Usually a culture establishes specific expectations for friendships, as with other essential social relationships such as those with spouse, parents, and children. If a friend dies we ought to attend his funeral, but in America there is no obligation requiring us to do so. When a man dies in West Africa, his friend must put on filthy rags and perform socially required rituals.

There exists an almost universal practice of gift exchange in different cultures. The practice is often socially required. In our Western culture this practice has declined in recent decades and is now largely reserved for family members. Americans still exchange Christmas card greetings and on occasion bring a token gift such as a bottle of wine when visiting the home of a friend or neighbor.

Why do people trade gifts that have only slight economic worth? The exchange of small gifts has symbolic rather than monetary significance. A major anthropological study of gift exchange concluded that presents are given to form and solidify closer relationships between individuals and groups.

On the surface, certain ceremonial behaviors may have little social significance, but the underlying social meaning and consequence is profound. Without the ritual and ceremony, and therefore the respect associated with friendship, we have few socially approved guidelines for developing friends. We are set adrift and must depend solely on a random process to get to know someone.

Robert Brain reports that on the continent of Africa today, cultural behavior among close friends is comparable to the David and Jonathan ideal. The Bangwa unashamedly sing their friends' praise. Public demonstration of friendship is common. At festivals they dance and sing. At funerals they express their grief through open weeping and even tear at their clothes over the loss of a close friend. The open display of happiness, grief, and other emotions contrasts with the American male's internalizing his God-given feelings, be they happy or sad. Of course there are cultural traits related to friendship norms throughout the world that would not be appealing or morally acceptable to us because of our upbringing or because they might violate a biblical mandate. But we can learn much from other ways of expressing friendship.

In the West, intimate friendships have been discouraged in favor of the close relationship between husband and wife. But it need not be an either/or relationship. In several Mediterranean countries, friendship is of significant emotional importance, as is the family and kinship system. The social fabric of the Alcala in Andalusia, an agricultural community, is bound together with friendship ties as strong and as important as those of kinship.

In numerous primitive societies, men must meet specific qualifications in order to become friends, and then adhere to stringent social rules to maintain the friendship. We, on the other hand, are hampered by our lack of societal ground rules about friendship conduct.

Jesus, in chapter 3 of Mark's Gospel, seems to extend—and even redefine—our kinship responsibilities and relationships to include friendship. During a conversation, a group of people told him that his mother and siblings were outside waiting for him. His response was, "Who is My mother, or My brothers?" Looking around the room he added, "Here are My mother and My brothers! For whoever does the will of God is My brother and My sister and mother" (vv. 31–35).

It is a myth that marriage alone can satisfy all of an individual's emotional needs. Without friends, a wife and husband must rely totally on each other for emotional support. Many Christian marriages collapse under the weight of this impossible demand. We should not expect our wives to meet all of our emotional needs. They cannot, nor were they created to do so.

The church should provide Christians with more than just the "how-to's" of marriage. The church must also encourage other long-term, supportive relationships where people can become grandparents, uncles, aunts, brothers, sisters—in other words, friends—to one another.

Intimacy and Culture

In every culture there is a need for intimate, trusting friendships. We all need individuals with whom we can be open and reveal our deepest feelings. There is something amiss with a culture that ignores or devalues the human bonds that are so important to our physical, psychological, and spiritual health and happiness.

Of course, we don't have to emulate friendship customs from cultures that differ significantly from our own any more than we should begin to wash dirt from people's feet as Jesus did for the disciples. Our culture and customs are different. Rather than copy friendship practices of other cultures, we should learn from them, and then within our own culture search for ways to practice biblical principles of friendship on a daily basis.

How can we do this? As you will see in the next chapter, we must begin with ourselves—you and me.

DISCUSSION QUESTIONS

1. How can cross-cultural information help us better understand the human nature God has given to us, including our need for friendship?
2. Why did Christ select only men as his closest friends and disciples?
3. Are male/female relationships different in the 1990s as some people claim? How does the move toward equality in the workplace affect relationships between men and women?
4. Is there an indication in your life that your desire for personal privacy and freedom is stronger than your desire for community and involvement in the lives of others?
5. How could friendship in the United States receive more social recognition similar to marriage and parenting roles? How about in your own life?

CHAPTER TEN

Understanding Yourself

The better part of one's life consists of his friend-ships.

—Abraham Lincoln

"**O**kay, I see the problem of my friendless condition and I understand the principles for meeting my friendship needs. But actually changing my behavior and thinking patterns is quite difficult." Reaching this point of awareness is the first step to improvement. Before progress can occur, one must believe that a problem exists and that progress is needed.

Acting on new knowledge frequently requires, first, the understanding of who we are today, and then, the unlearning, by daily application of biblical principles, of what we previously were taught. To understand ourselves is difficult. Self-examination is a personal and sometimes painful exercise. Plato said, "The unexamined life is not worth living." Most of us, however, would just as soon forego objective introspection.

But there are no shortcuts to personal change and growth. Don't be discouraged. Knowledge and personal examination provide the base for action. **133**

The Bible defines much of life as a process of becoming. We push toward the mark. We grow in grace. We begin as babes in Christ. There are no shortcuts to growth; but the process, getting from where we are to where we want to go, can be enjoyable.

Caution: Assimilating biblical principles takes time. Once a problem is identified, it is the nature of the American male to want an immediate solution. But if we fail to change at the core of our personality, our thinking will not be altered and our new behavior will be contrived. Sooner or later, and more likely sooner, we will backslide into old patterns.

You can, however, successfully apply biblical principles and thereby develop quality relationships with others. Sure, it's difficult to look within and ask why we act and think as we do. "Am I afraid? Am I a bigot? Am I hateful? Am I impatient? Am I selfish? Am I arrogant? Am I comfortable in my self-sufficiency?" But we must ask these and other uncomfortable questions of ourselves, and answer them objectively, one by one, in the context of our everyday lives if we're to change for the better.

Ingrained Prejudices

I attended an educational meeting last spring. Methods for educating talented and gifted children are being looked at closely within my own school corporation, and I was quite pleased to learn that this topic was going to be considered at one of the sessions. Arriving a few minutes early, I settled in, anticipating a useful lecture on education of the gifted. But sometimes we learn more than we want to in a situation.

The elementary school teacher who spoke to our group was a young, attractive, well-dressed woman. When I learned she was the speaker, my initial thought was,

"What could she know about gifted education at the high school and college levels?" However, it was really too late to get up and leave; besides, it would have been rude.

I'm glad I remained. She was intelligent and quite knowledgeable about the neglected topic of how best to teach brilliant children. Much of what she said was useful for the level of student I worked with as well.

Why then was I turned off before I gave her a chance? I have always told my children, Julie and Cameron, "Don't make snap judgments; give people a chance; don't be prejudiced." And yet it was I who was prejudiced. Maybe it was because she was young—"What does she know, she's only a kid." Deep down maybe I also held the prejudiced view that an attractive woman is rarely very intelligent. Maybe I would have responded the same way to a less attractive woman—because she was a woman. (Am I really a chauvinist?) And then there was the fact that she represented the lower elementary grades. Whatever the cause of my quickly formed, unfair stereotype, I was dead wrong.

Many of us men must admit that we often make snap judgments and then, mentally or physically or both, we withdraw from someone who could be a true friend. We've got to break the habit of rapidly forming first impressions. If you find you are making quick, categorical conclusions about someone, ask yourself, "Why am I reacting this way toward this person?" Bringing your values to a conscious level helps you avoid being unjust or distorting reality.

Incidentally, first impressions, once formed, are rather difficult to change, even when confronted with new information that conflicts with the unfair stereotype. Don't do it—don't make unfair snap judgments about another person's intelligence, knowledge, character, personality, spirituality, or motives. You may wound another person's spirit or self-confidence and, at the same time, starve yourself from the needed nutrition that comes from involvement with others. The Bible very clearly states, for example in James 2, that prejudice is sin.

It's extremely difficult to uproot ingrained prejudices once established. When we acquire prejudices, we tend unconsciously to defend them in the face of facts that contradict our beliefs.

Discovering my prejudice was only part of what I learned from the teacher who hosted the workshop. Soon after she began, she divided us into small groups. She wanted us to work together on a project that would help us learn more about gifted kids. Well, it did fulfill its intended purpose, but I learned something else as well. The women in our seminar were more eager to work together and to share ideas. I honestly felt a little uncomfortable working with others and depending on them to complete the assigned activity.

Like most men I am used to working alone. We tend to believe that our greatest successes come from individual and independent efforts on some task. I remember few occasions in my college or graduate school experiences where I was put in a situation similar to this workshop for the gifted. My formal learning experiences were based on competition with classmates, not cooperation.

After I got beyond the uncomfortable feeling in the small group to which I was assigned, I thoroughly enjoyed the learning experience. The adage "If you want a job done right, do it yourself" is not always true. We must not shrink from social, religious, or work-related activities that bring us into contact with other people.

Isolation in Moderation

Self-imposed psychological and/or physical isolation is good only in moderation. Don't try to do everything by yourself. The author of the following humorous account is unknown. I'm sure you'll agree that it illustrates our need at times to accept the help of others.

Dear Sir:

I am writing in response to your request for more information concerning Block #11 on the insurance form which asks for "cause of injuries" wherein I put "Trying to do the job alone." You said you needed more information so I trust the following will be sufficient.

I am a bricklayer by trade, and on the date of injuries I was working alone laying brick around the top of a four-story building when I realized that I had about 500 pounds of brick left over. Rather than carry the bricks down by hand, I decided to put them into a barrel and lower them by a pulley which was fastened to the top of the building. I secured the end of the rope at ground level and went up to the top of the building and loaded the bricks into the barrel and swung the barrel out with the bricks in it. I then went down and untied the rope, holding it securely to insure the slow descent of the barrel.

As you will note on Block #6 of the insurance form, I weigh 145 pounds. Due to my shock at being jerked off the ground so swiftly, I lost my presence of mind and forgot to let go of the rope. Between the second and third floors I met the barrel coming down. This accounts for the bruises and lacerations on my upper body.

Regaining my presence of mind again, I held tightly to the rope and proceeded rapidly up the side of the building, not stopping until my right hand was jammed in the pulley. This accounts for the broken thumb.

Despite the pain, I retained my presence of mind and held tightly to the rope. At approximately the same time, however, the barrel of bricks hit the ground and the bottom fell out of the barrel. Devoid of the weight of the bricks, the barrel now weighed about 50 pounds. I again refer you to Block #6 and my weight.

As you would guess, I began a rapid descent. In the vicinity of the second floor I met the barrel coming up. This explains the injuries to my legs and lower body. Slowed only slightly, I continued my descent, landing on the pile of bricks. This accounts for my sprained back and internal injuries.

I am sorry to report, however, that at this point, I again lost my presence of mind and let go of the rope, and as you can imagine, the empty barrel crashed down on me. This accounts for my head injuries.

I trust this answers your concern. Please know that I am finished "trying to do the job alone."

If we would just reach out and ask for help, we could avoid many difficulties and accomplish more in the process.

Importance of Touch

Although an abundance of research exists that men need both to give and to receive physical affection, rarely does a man express his feelings physically. We do not touch. Touching of any kind implies sex to most men. If they are not engaged in contact on the football field or engrossed in sexual intercourse, American men will not touch other humans, especially men. We are afraid. We have been conditioned to believe that expressing emotions is wrong.

Andrew M. Greeley, in his book *The Friendship Game*, argues that fear is the major barrier to friendship. I must agree. Even within the church we see people sitting together—alone. We smile, we may even say hello, but we don't know one another.

Our behavior at church is similar to being on an elevator. We don't stand too close to anyone else; we don't talk; we look straight ahead; and we can hardly wait for the door to open so we can run out. Being at church can be like one more meeting in the usual Monday through Friday experience. But it should be different.

Solitary worship is easy, for it demands nothing of us. How different the contemporary American church is from the ideal established by Jesus. In John 13, Jesus says that people will know that we belong to him if we have love for each other. Over the past several years, many evangelical leaders have called us to recapture caring, open, sharing relationships within the body of Christians. Leaders in this relational theology movement include Bruce Larson *(Dare to Live, Living on the Growing Edge)*, Keith Miller *(Taste of New Wine)*, and Larry Crabb *(Inside Out)*. Don't blame others if things are not as you wish. As the Bell telephone ad used to say, "Reach out and touch someone."

Before beginning a recent Saturday morning shopping venture, my family and I had breakfast in an Indianapolis restaurant. While we were eating, Sue Ann drew my attention to something unusual. Two cars had pulled up to the curb together. A family of five or six piled out of each car. Everyone began talking to each other. There were smiles and handshakes all around. This was a pleasant sight, but not all that unusual. As we were watching what must have been a family reunion, two of the men actually hugged each other unashamedly, and then walked into the restaurant continuing to talk with arms around each other's shoulders.

As we were leaving, I couldn't resist the temptation to find out why these two men were so affectionate. They were glad to talk with me but had not thought much about the display of their feelings. The men were brothers, raised by an affectionate mother who had not instructed her sons to internalize all of their feelings.

Maybe you didn't have such an upbringing and you still keep most or all of your feelings to yourself. It's never too late to change. Whom do you care about? Do they know how you feel about them? It's high time you tell them before it's too late. Some men, due to childhood training, believe they cannot physically show how they feel, especially to another man. Each of us, however, has the ability and the need to tell other people how we feel about them. Sure you can be discreet, and the time should be appropriate, but the point is, don't let a relationship suffer or die because of poor communication.

When notified that his father was dying in a Los Angeles hospital, the son flew across country to be with his dad. During his vigil at his father's bed, it suddenly struck him that he had never in his entire life told his father he loved him. Nor had he hugged him or cried with him anytime in his forty-six years of being a son. He wanted desperately and belatedly to hug, to cry, to say "I love you," but his father never regained a fully conscious state. Another lifetime of opportunity was missed because of our cult of manliness.

I greatly value the relationship I have with my eleven-year-old son. I want him to know that I love him and always will. I don't want there to be any doubt in his mind. I demonstrate my love to him in small ways such as working on his go-cart engine with him, fishing together at the creek near our home, or making a snowman and snowballs together.

Last year Cameron's fourth-grade teacher assigned him and the rest of his class a creative writing project. My son wrote a paragraph about our relationship that touched my heart. With his permission, I share it with you.

> I admire my Dad. I admire him because he cares for me and loves me. He reads Narnia to me and we have lots of laughter and we wonder. Dr. C. S. Lewis wrote the book. My Dad and I play football and tag. We built a fort. It cost about $150. We put shingles on the roof. It didn't have any leaks in it. There were some bugs. My Dad is real special to me.

Relationships between fathers and sons, however, are not always close. In fact, physical and emotional estrangement between sons and their fathers is such a common occurrence that it has become a popular topic. Men are writing and speaking about it. The popular country singer Kenny Rogers has spoken out about the lost six years in which he failed to even speak to his son Kenny, Jr. In an article about the need fathers and sons have for each other,[1] former President Reagan's son admits, "I have spent my life trying to figure out how to make Ronald Reagan my friend." How much we lose as fathers when we fail to befriend our sons. How much we lose as sons when our fathers fail to befriend us.

We learn much from our fathers about the value and development of male friendships. What did your father teach you? What are you teaching your son? Do you have a relationship to restore? If so, what are you waiting for?

Be Strong Enough to Cry!

Sue and I were married on a muggy August afternoon in South Bend, Indiana, in 1965. Even before that date, we had talked about how many children we wanted for our family. Did we want a boy first or a girl? We decided it didn't really matter. Then we discussed how far apart we would space them. If this weren't naive enough, we also talked of what month we should conceive. If she became pregnant in, say, September, our baby would be born in the spring, which we thought would be an ideal time.

Well, so much for well-intentioned plans. The years came and went. We remained childless, but not for a lack of trying. We saw a urologist and a fertility specialist. Sue took a fertility drug faithfully for three or four years. Still no baby.

We lived in a young married, family-oriented neighborhood. Sue became bored and even angry with the incessant talk about children and birth and labor experiences. And late at night she cried. Her tears expressed her desire for motherhood. Being a typical man, I felt uncomfortable when on occasion she expressed her emotion. As I think back, I believe I was actually uncomfortable with my feelings rather than Sue's. How does a man act? What could I say or do? I guess I wanted to appear strong when I too was hurting.

Following much prayer we agreed (it was easy for me) that Sue would undergo an operation. It was like an answer to prayer. Sue became pregnant a few months later. It seemed so right. We had been married over seven years, had worked as youth leaders in the church, and wanted young people of our own. Besides, we informed God during our innumerable petitions that we had indeed learned the patience he must obviously intend for us to acquire.

All that waiting and frustration were now behind us, or so we thought. It was the middle of the night when Sue awakened me. "Something is wrong. We'd better call the doctor." The rest of the night and following two days were spent in the hospital. We lost our child whom we had grown to love during his five months of development in Sue's body.

I didn't cry. An attending physician told me, "Be strong

so you can help your wife. She's emotional right now." But it was I rather than my wife who was acting abnormally. She was expressing her grief and sense of loss in a normal fashion and found it difficult to understand why I didn't cry. I knew the Bible doesn't tell us it is wrong to sorrow. After all, Jesus wept openly and unashamedly at the grave of his friend Lazarus.

I returned home to pack a bag for Sue and make a few phone calls. At home in total solitude I finally wept. Today I know those tears were good for me, for they helped to release the emotional buildup of anger, resentment, and sense of loss. It would have been better if they had been shared with Sue, but at the time I felt ashamed. When I called my mother, the strong male image I had wished to maintain simply collapsed.

Sue convalesced at home for several days. It was during this time that I was finally able to reveal my emotions by talking and crying with Sue. We planned a week's trip together. This sharing and planning did much to begin the healing of our hearts. I, as much as Sue, needed to talk about what had happened.

I can't remember a story more significant about the importance of admitting that we men must reveal our emotions than this letter published in a 1986 Ann Landers column:[2]

Dear Ann Landers:

Something happened to me recently that tore me apart.

I made my first visit to the Vietnam Memorial looking for Robert Williamson's name. He was my buddy in a unit near Pleiku, where he died in January 1968.

The polished marble with all those names and the variety of flowers got to me. I was fighting to keep my composure when I heard someone say "Robert Williamson."

In front of me stood a man and a woman with two children. The man was holding up one of the children to touch the name.

I wanted to speak to them and find out how they were related. It could have been a meaningful and heartwarming experience but I was afraid to show my emotions. I knew I would break down and cry, so I walked away.

Since then I have relived that incident thousands of times thinking of what I should have done, but of course it's too late.

Please tell your readers not to be ashamed to show their emotions. I realize now that I wouldn't have been the first Vietnam veteran to cry at that monument and I won't have been the last.

Sincerely,
Ken Anderson
Oregon, Wisconsin

This embarrassed veteran urges each of us to show our emotions. He understands now that it is not an emotion of weakness.

We need to learn to grieve and to share our grief with others. If we fail to express our emotional feelings, I'm convinced our lives will be lonely and possibly shortened. And we probably won't be much comfort to others either.

The Necessity of Risk

To share your thoughts, fears, and dreams openly with the crowd is to risk being labeled foolish. A reviewer of my first book, writing in the *Los Angeles Times,* called me naive. I think he disagreed with my Christian worldview, but I admit I felt hurt by the criticism.

But we should not let fear of criticism stop us from

trying to enter into the lives of others. More than criticism, we should fear loneliness, meaninglessness, and missed opportunities for service to others. Whenever you reach out to another person, you take a chance of being rejected. Leo Buscaglia comments, "To love is to risk not being loved in return [but] I don't love to be loved in return."

Buscaglia continues, "To hope is to risk despair and to try is to risk failure. But risk must be taken, because the greatest risk in life is to risk nothing. The person who risks nothing, does nothing, has nothing."[3] Buscaglia is right. A man may avoid suffering and sorrow, but he simply cannot learn and feel and change and grow apart from risk. Chained by his attitudes, he's a slave. He's forfeited his freedom. Only the person who risks is truly free.

In a similar spirit, C. S. Lewis wrote:

> To love at all is to be vulnerable. Love anything, and your heart will certainly be wrung and possibly broken. If you want to make sure of keeping it intact, you must give your heart to no one, not even to an animal. Wrap it carefully round with hobbies and little luxuries: avoid all entanglements; lock it up safe in the casket or coffin of your selfishness. But in that casket—safe, dark, motionless, airless—it will change. It will not be broken: instead, it will become unbreakable, impenetrable, irredeemable.[4]

A few years ago Harvard University conducted a study of millionaires. The results of this study may surprise you. You may not be able to predict who is or will be a millionaire based upon intelligence, education, or even family background. Of course, successful people tend to acquire more education and tend to be intelligent. But these traits were not the only predictors of significant wealth. The Harvard study found the following characteristics to be very common among millionaires:

- They find good in others.
- They have self-confidence.
- They are enthusiastic.
- They appreciate humor.

All of us can cultivate these traits in our professional and personal lives. To internalize these traits will make us better individuals, which is more important than acquiring wealth.

Assessing Yourself

This chapter ends with the following friendship inventory. Please invest a few minutes to fill in your responses. Your responses will be especially useful when you read the next chapter, which will continue the discussion about risk-taking and goal-setting. Your answers will help you identify those areas of your life that may be weak and hampering your success at making or maintaining friendships.

FRIENDSHIP INVENTORY

	USUALLY	SOMETIMES	NEVER
SPIRITUAL FOCUS			
I'm concerned with the spirituality of the men I know.	☐	☐	☐
I'm able to talk about Christ and the Bible with friends.	☐	☐	☐
I pray with and for my friends.	☐	☐	☐
The activities I share with friends are wholesome.	☐	☐	☐
COVENANT			
I remember important occasions and celebrate them with letters, cards, or calls.	☐	☐	☐
I'm not afraid to risk being rejected by reaching out to another.	☐	☐	☐
My friends know by my words and actions that they are important to me.	☐	☐	☐
I try to heal strained or broken relationships.	☐	☐	☐
I honor my commitments to my friends.	☐	☐	☐
FAITHFULNESS/LOYALTY			
My friends can count on me.	☐	☐	☐
I can keep a confidence.	☐	☐	☐
I take full responsibility for what I do and say.	☐	☐	☐
I am not a fair-weather friend.	☐	☐	☐
I keep in touch with friends who now are separated from me by miles.	☐	☐	☐
SOCIAL INVOLVEMENT			
I enjoy making new friends and ask questions to learn more about them.	☐	☐	☐

	Usually	**Sometimes**	**Never**
I greet new acquaintances warmly.	☐	☐	☐
I don't begrudge the giving of my time or money when I see a needy person or cause.	☐	☐	☐
I plant shade trees under which I know I'll never sit. (I'm not selfish.)	☐	☐	☐
I'm a good neighbor—I do not criticize others.	☐	☐	☐
I do not discriminate against men who are of a different race, ethnic group, religion, or social class.	☐	☐	☐

CANDOR

I speak the truth in love.	☐	☐	☐
I am honest in my relationships.	☐	☐	☐
I'm not defensive if a friend talks about a problem in my life.	☐	☐	☐
I can ask for help if I'm in need.	☐	☐	☐

RESPECT

I believe God loves each individual.	☐	☐	☐
I am tactful, considerate, and do not take advantage of close friends.	☐	☐	☐
I express gratitude when I've been helped by someone.	☐	☐	☐
I have a deep-seated belief in the inherent worth of myself and others.	☐	☐	☐
I respect the right of each of my friends to be different from me.	☐	☐	☐

ACCEPTANCE

I am not judgmental of the behavior and thinking of others.	☐	☐	☐
Material things or status are not important in my relationships.	☐	☐	☐
I look for the good in others and minimize their faults.	☐	☐	☐
I express specific and honest appreciations.	☐	☐	☐
I don't hold grudges.	☐	☐	☐

	Usually	Sometimes	Never
EMPATHY			
People I know experience God's love through me.	☐	☐	☐
I sincerely try to understand how other people feel and think. (I invest the time needed to accomplish this.)	☐	☐	☐
I do not force my views on other people.	☐	☐	☐
I treat other people as equals.	☐	☐	☐
LISTENING			
I take the time needed to listen to others.	☐	☐	☐
I listen for the feeling in people's words.	☐	☐	☐
I don't talk too much or interrupt people when they talk.	☐	☐	☐
I ask men questions about their own lives.	☐	☐	☐
I listen alertly and avoid distractions.	☐	☐	☐
SELF-DISCLOSURE			
I do not try to act like someone I'm not. (I am genuine.)	☐	☐	☐
My friends and I confide in each other.	☐	☐	☐
I'm willing to reveal a weakness or ask for help from a friend.	☐	☐	☐
I don't fear sharing my emotions.	☐	☐	☐
COMPROMISE			
I don't have to have things my way.	☐	☐	☐
I do not expect my friends to be perfect.	☐	☐	☐
When wrong, I admit it. (I also say, "I'm sorry.")	☐	☐	☐
I deal with conflicting ideas with reason and understanding.	☐	☐	☐
I do not have a competitive, win-or-lose orientation that makes life a succession of contests.	☐	☐	☐
I adapt to new conditions in a spirit of cooperation.	☐	☐	☐

DISCUSSION QUESTIONS

1. Based on the friendship inventory, what roadblocks prevent you from making friends?
2. What small steps can you take to begin work on the problem areas?
3. Do hugging, crying, or other outward expressions of affection make you feel uncomfortable? Why?
4. In what ways are you like the bricklayer who attempted to do the job alone?
5. Do you enjoy the daily process of personal growth, or are you living in either the past or the future?
6. What causes prejudice and what can be done to prevent or remove it? Has prejudice hindered you from forming friendships with certain individuals?

CHAPTER ELEVEN

Setting Goals for Change

A trip of a thousand miles begins with the first step.
—Chinese proverb

I don't know how they count our brain cells, but neurosurgeons tell us we have four billion of them. This wonderful, miraculous personal computer is available to help us accomplish our dreams. But even with a great resource like the human brain, we need the belief that we can succeed. In fact, the positive belief in self is the one most significant element in success. If you think you can or if you think you can't, you're probably right.

Track fans said it was impossible to break the four-minute mile. Roger Banister was confident he could break this physical and psychological barrier. He did it! And soon after the barrier was broken, others followed with marks under four minutes.

In the film *Chariots of Fire*, Eric Liddell is bumped off the track and falls while running in competition. But he gets up, runs that much harder—and wins!

Do you have the sense of being in a race? Do you have clearly identified goals that give life meaning and push you forward into the future? What goal draws you onward? *Significant accomplishments are made by ordinary people with a focused task.*

Nehemiah wrote, "Let us arise and build" (Neh. 2:18). He knew his task was to build a wall and he did it. I like that. Change is possible when we have goals.

We must believe in ourselves and our own potential whether we are encouraged by significant others or not. If you wait around for others to encourage you to action, you may not change.

When Walt Disney began to work with animation, he experienced discouragement not only from skeptical bankers but also from his father. His dad told Walt he ought to "learn a real trade." But Walt Disney believed in himself and his new ideas about fantasy and entertainment. Disney used four words that reveal his confidence and motivation: *think, believe, dream,* and *dare.*

With little more than a dream, he launched a new industry that has touched millions of us. The four words that gave him hope can be our words too as we work to build more satisfying relationships with other men.

Norman Vincent Peale tells a story that took place in Cincinnati when he was about ten years old. The young Peale and his father were walking on the street when a dirty elderly man in tattered clothing approached, pulled on the boy's sleeve, and said, "Young man, give me something." Dr. Peale remembers that when he shook the man away, it greatly displeased his father. Norman attempted to defend his action with, "But, Dad, he's a bum." His father responded, "There is no such thing as a bum. There may be some people who haven't made the most of their lives, but all of us are still children of God."

Peale was admonished to go back to the man, give him a dollar, and wish him a Merry Christmas. Quickly he followed his father's instructions. The surprised old man said, "I thank you, young sir. Merry Christmas." Dr. Peale remembers, "In that moment his face became almost beautiful to me. He was no longer a bum."[1]

The elderly man had not changed. To the young Peale, the man was no longer a bum because he had, with his father's encouragement, gotten closer to another person.

A few years ago newspapers across America reported that a nurse and her two children kept a dead husband and father for eight long years in the bed he died in. They changed his linen every few days and attempted to go on with life pretending he was still alive. We, of course, find this bizarre. And yet ordinary people like you and me are often willing to nurse dead ideas, dead religion, dead behavior, and dead values. We resist change even when God wants us to change, even when we know in our hearts it's in our best interest to change.

Facing Our Fears

During the Great Depression, Franklin D. Roosevelt said, "The only thing we have to fear is fear itself." Our fears, often unconscious, tend to paralyze us, preventing the possibility of change. "God hath not given us the spirit of fear; but . . . of a sound mind" (2 Tim. 1:7 KJV). We have, therefore, the ability to deal with our fears rationally, logically, prayerfully as we lean on the support of God and those who love us. Fear, squarely faced, tends to ebb in significance. In John Bunyan's nineteenth-century classic *Pilgrim's Progress*, Christian's path was beset by alarming shapes that scuttled about in the shifting mists. These sinister monsters proved to be tiny creatures unable to hurt anyone. You need to realize that your fear is unnecessary. To paraphrase Philippians 4:6, "Don't be uptight about this. Rather, ask God to help you with your fears."

Several years ago *Decision* magazine told the story of Shoichi Yokoi, a World War II Japanese soldier. For twenty-eight years following the war, Shoichi Yokoi lived as a hermit in a cave on the island of Guam. He and several like him ignored pamphlets dropped from planes that announced the end of the war. Rather than take the risk of possible imprisonment, he chose to live in a self-imposed prison of his own making and thus gave up years of freedom.[2] We find this hard to believe and yet many of us men live in caves of emotionlessness and lack of intimacy that is largely self-inflicted.

If you are to break out of your cave, you must break through to other men in short, small stages. As you do, your fears will ebb. Explore ideas and, later, feelings with them. Ask their opinions and be willing to share a few of your own. By asking their thoughts on a topic, you send out the subtle message that you recognize and respect them as individuals. William James, the influential psychologist of the early 1900s, said, "The deepest principle of man is the craving to be appreciated."

When I was teaching high school and college social studies classes, I required students to prepare a research paper on a problem or issue in American society. Part of the assignment was to interview two individuals who were directly involved in some way with the subject matter of the paper. To be sure, this assignment was not often received with enthusiasm. Students feared that the men and women they wanted to interview would resent giving them time. These students were also afraid they would ask dumb questions.

We discovered that, with few exceptions, those interviewed were very willing to talk with students. Some of them even called me to offer to speak to the entire class or just to say thanks for the opportunity to share. They were glad to take the time to share because someone asked their opinion.

The students sent thank-you notes and reported enthusiastically that it was a good experience. Similar to these kids, we men need to ask questions and take an interest in others. Fear is unnecessary. Usually you'll be pleasantly surprised when you befriend others.

You Can Change!

God's help and your own resolve provide the best combination for change known to man. Your own inner strength is more powerful than you might at first realize. The Lord has given each of us various gifts and talents that he intends for us to use. D. L. Moody once said that if your house is burning, don't pray about it, put the fire out. There is truth to the criticism that some Christians act so heavenly they are of no earthly good. It is not a contradiction to depend upon God and yourself at the same time. You realize that God is the ultimate source of your strength, and at the same time, that you are personally responsible for what you do and say.

You must believe in yourself and in your ability to change. Don't meditate on past defeats as many men do. Even in areas of your life where you have experienced failure, the correct response is not "I can't do this." With this attitude you'll *never* be able to do whatever "this" might be. A more appropriate response is "With God's help, I'll turn this failure into victory" or "I haven't yet but I'm working on it." In the book *How to Be Your Own Best Friend,* the authors suggest, "If we all just kept on doing exactly what we've done up to now, people would never change, and people are changing all the time. That's what growth is—doing what you've never done before."

On my desk at home I have a card which reads, "You Are What You Do, Not What You Say You'll Do." This reminder helps me to overcome one of my persistent weaknesses—impatience. A friend told me I should ask God for patience and tell him I want it right now! What roadblocks in your life are preventing you from fully participating in a more useful, abundant life? What patterns of thought or behavior now separate you from applying biblical principles of friendship?

One secret of success in changing long-standing patterns is first, to concentrate on specific items that need change, and, second, to strive for small improvements. The trip of a thousand miles begins with a single step. Begin small. As you create and achieve realistic short-range goals, sooner or later you'll enjoy significant improvements.

What now prevents you from making biblical principles and positive personality traits part of your life? Refer to the Friendship Inventory at the end of the last chapter. Your responses should help you identify problems to work on.

After you have selected certain items from the inventory that you feel are definite problems in the way you think or behave, focus your attention in these areas. For each item that you marked as "Never," ask, "Why is this a problem? Where am I right now with this problem? What is my goal? And how do I get from where I am to where I want to be?" Set goals for yourself and list in small, manageable steps how you'll accomplish the desired end result.

In the final analysis you cannot say that you are what you are because society has taught you to be macho, or your parents raised you incorrectly, or you were converted too early or too late in life, or you're a man, or because of any other external factor. To allow yourself to be controlled by external variables is to become little more than a robot. *You are what you are because you have chosen to be what you are. You are the person in control of your life.*

The Freudians have given us much insight into the human mind but they err on this critical point. You are responsible to God and other humans for your behavior because you are relatively free to act as you please.

In 1989 a gang of New York teenagers nearly killed a jogger in Central Park because "they felt like it." One New York columnist blamed society for the vicious attack rather than the teenagers themselves. Many columnists, including George Will, fired back that to blame society was nonsense. If we are to remain civilized, individuals must be responsible for their own behavior, circumstances notwithstanding. We are not puppets on strings, totally controlled by social and psychological forces.

Edward O. Wilson, in his controversial book *Social Biology*, states otherwise, however. He claims that our behavior is the result of how we were raised *and* how our genes were programmed. In virtually every field of social science today, and now also in the natural sciences, man is viewed as a machine. Machines, of course, are not responsible for their behavior and are useful only if they can produce something valued by the culture. Machines are disposable and lack morals or intrinsic value.

This is not the Bible's view of man. We are not a *tabula rasa* or a mindless lump of clay to be molded by others. How much control do I really have over my own life? Can I change on my own or do I need counseling to improve my patterns of living? In some cases we can engage in self-examination on a solo basis. Self-reflection and contemplation are always helpful. But many men need the added insights, understanding, and objectivity that can be provided only by an outsider such as a close friend, wife, or even a counselor.

When I mention therapy, what comes to your mind? Most evangelicals shun the term, associating it with Freudian psychology and psychoanalysis. John Warwick

Montgomery says we should be morally offended by Sigmund Freud's explaining God away as a mythical father figure. Christians, says Montgomery, should explain Freud away as a product of his own neurosis. Freud had serious emotional problems himself (as did his disciple Carl Jung) and admitted he had little interest in helping suffering humanity, only in understanding it. Accepting without examination the tenets of modern psychology is obviously dangerous.

A 1988 Brown University study found what many of us social scientists knew already: A courtroom decision based on flipping a coin can be as accurate as one based on the judgment of a psychologist. Professor David Faust concluded that there is virtually no evidence that psychologists are any better equipped to make judgments or assess the psychological conditions of dependents than are lay individuals.

Where can we find counseling help if we reject the beliefs of psychoanalysis? After all, emotional pain is a real phenomenon. Fortunately, most emotional problems can be alleviated if another person is willing to invest both concern and time in our well-being. O. Quentin Hyder, M.D., writes:

> This is the key to good psychology and counseling—to care, to really care, and to let the sufferer know that you care. If more Christians made themselves available in this way to help the weaker brother and sister in need when the troubles first started, there would be far fewer numbers of them having to go later for professional help. The burden of my message is that caring Christians can significantly contribute to the mental and emotional health of their fellow church members and Christian friends. To do so we must make ourselves available and give time and our own emotional energies and resources to succor those in need.[3]

People with serious adjustment problems should consult an evangelical pastor, one who knows biblically based professional counselors. I would also suggest reading William Glasser, *Reality Therapy*; Albert Ellis, *A New Guide to Rational Living*; Paul Tournier, *The Healing of Persons*; C. S. Lewis, *The Problem of Pain*; Cecil Osborne, *The Art of Understanding Your Mate*; Frank Minirth et al., *Love Is a Choice*; and Chris Thurman, *The Lies We Believe.*[4]

In most cases you can change without the use of professional help. Christ can free you from your old negative lifestyle patterns (2 Cor. 5:17) and provide you with what is good for both you and those around you (Gal. 5:22,23; 2 Pet. 1:5–7). You are the person in control of your life. With God at your side, begin now to change how you think and how you behave. Don't put it off. No day is a bad day to begin.

Our greatest problem is not other people but rather ourselves. Remember the *Pogo* quote at the beginning of Chapter 3—"We have met the enemy and he is us"? In the Galatian letter (5:17) Paul records that for the Christian, one's human nature and spiritual nature are in dire conflict. What we need is help. Good intentions, no matter how pure, like New Year's resolutions, rarely result in long-term changed attitudes and behavior. You need your own resolve and dedication to be sure; but one additional step is also needed—without the support of God, changes, if they occur at all, are usually cosmetic as well as short-lived.

"Let God change you inwardly" (Rom. 12:2 TEV). J. B. Phillips translates this verse, "Let God remold your minds from within."

DISCUSSION QUESTIONS

1. Set three realistic short-term goals for yourself. Write them down along with specific steps needed to help you reach your goals.
2. What are the barriers that could block your progress toward accomplishing these goals? How can the identified roadblocks best be overcome?
3. Why do we resist positive change even when we know it is in our best interest? What can you do to minimize your fears of change and fears of rejection?
4. William Glasser's reality therapy argues that we as individuals are responsible for our own behavior. Discuss his view in light of the teaching of the Bible. To what degree are we really responsible for our own individual actions and thoughts? How should this impact your approach to change?
5. How can God help you change? What can you do in your relationship with Him to pave the way for self-improvement?

CHAPTER TWELVE

Confronting American Culture

Do not conform any longer to the pattern of this world, but be transformed by the renewing of your mind. Then you will be able to test and approve what God's will is.

—Romans 12:2 NIV

During the nineteenth century the United States was mainly a rural and agricultural nation. Most families lived on farms in sparsely populated areas. Work and other activities were done together by all members of the family. The wife, husband, and children all shared the tasks of producing what the family itself consumed.

As the country developed into an industrial nation, sex roles became more rigid. Usually it was the man who left the home and the farm to earn a living in town. Children left home to attend school. Women remained in the home to care for small children and household duties. Roles became more sharply defined. But during World War II, hundreds of thousands of American women left home to enter the factories in an attempt to help with the war effort.

Following the war, for economic and social reasons, many women remained in the work force, and many men married and went to college on the GI **161** bill. With wives working full time and husbands in school, less of a stigma existed for males who shared domestic chores of laundry, shopping, and cleaning. Our culture began to change its definition again of male or female behavior. But we have not yet redefined maleness so that men can express their feelings and fears and conform to biblical norms. For example, we're still suspicious of a man who spends too much time caring for children. Nor can a man be too understanding or emotional if he wants to avoid raised eyebrows.

Frontier Ethic

Despite the significant changes in this and the last century, many men still adhere to what I would call a frontier ethic, a throwback to the eighteenth and nineteenth centuries. They still exalt the image of the powerful autonomous men of the wild West. In the shoot-out at the OK Corral, one could not afford to be second-best. On the frontier combating the elements, starvation, disease, wild animals, and Indians, a man *had* to win. First place was all that was available. To lose was to die.

While the frontier disappeared a century ago, many still cling to a frontier mentality. The frontier behavior and thinking which served earlier generations in their struggles with physical survival is an anachronism today. We still feel that finishing first is vital to our masculinity, to our emotional survival. During the seventies the Minnesota Vikings won many football play-off championships, but were relegated by the press to the loser category since they failed to win "the big one." The big one, of course, is the Super Bowl, currently America's most important annual pageant. The San Francisco Giants got the same treatment in the late fifties and sixties. The Dallas Cowboys also had a great string of play-off victories in the sixties. What was said of this winning team? They too couldn't win the big one. We're told that heated competition makes winners, and so it does. But it makes many more non-winners.

Every athlete should do his or her best. Dodger pitcher Orel Hershiser says in his book *Out of the Blue* that as a Christian he is obligated to the best he can do. To do otherwise would be hypocrisy or passive acceptance of defeat. High standards and devotion to a task are important, but they are not to be confused with winning at any cost or assuming that losing a contest makes one a failure. Unfortunately, we tend to value only winners.

Neil Armstrong was the first man on the moon. Who was second? Who was vice president (second place) in the administrations of Washington, Jefferson, Lincoln, Wilson, Roosevelt, or Kennedy? Even in more recent days, many would be hard pressed to identify the vice-presidents in the Carter, Reagan, or Bush administrations. We're told, although incorrectly, that Columbus was first to discover America. Who was second? The second man to fly solo across the Atlantic was as daring as Charles Lindbergh, but no one ever hears of him.

Might makes right today as well as it did on the frontier. Money and power make even a sleazy character like Al Capone important. The frontier ethic of being first at all costs is only one anachronistic legacy that still plagues our culture's view of the way American males must perform in the 1990s.

Social Darwinism

In the 1880s a new philosophy was popularized, partially to justify an emerging ruthlessness in business, but also to explain why only a few were winners in the competitive game of life. Those with great wealth needed some way philosophically to numb the guilt they felt when they surveyed the desperate poverty endured by the multitudes.

Rather than attempt to create a more equitable means to distribute income, many of the rich sought a system to explain why the poor were to blame for their own misery. A new philosophy was needed to blame the victim for his condition and thus remove personal responsibility and the need for correct action.

Using the biological theories developed by Charles Darwin in the 1850s, the English philosopher Herbert Spencer, and others, developed the idea of *social Darwinism*. The disparity of very rich and very poor was the result of the iron laws of nature. The rich, and many of the poor themselves, believed or at least supported the argument that fixed laws of nature existed to guide human conduct. Nature was vicious, not beneficient, and survival of the fittest was the law for human behavior as well as for the animal world. The poor and handicapped were viewed as unfit and expendable since nature was attempting to better each species.

Therefore, if you had great wealth it was not due to a gift from your parents or God, but rather because you were superior to other creatures and were meant to lord it over lesser men as some powerful animals control or destroy their prey. Natural selection, not divine providence, reigned supreme.

This thinking encouraged the American psyche to drift far from the Christian world view which, illustrated in Jesus, elevates the values of gentleness, concern, and sensitivity for others. Rather than destroy or explain away the weak, Jesus was compassionate and offered help. His discussion of the good Samaritan will forever stand as a beacon of hope for the downtrodden and also as a challenge for those who have the capacity to reach out to the less fortunate. He came to serve others (Matt. 20:28). Jesus had time for people, even so-called unimportant people like the woman at the well. He touched people like the leper (Luke 5:12–13) and wasn't too concerned if others thought he was doing the wrong thing according to the cultural values of the time. And he wanted to spend time with children (Mark 10:13–16). These traits are not exactly valued in our contemporary culture.

The narrow American belief in self-reliance, strength, courage, independence, and winning at the exclusion of other values and realities has taken a heavy toll on modern man. Author Horatio Alger perpetuated the myth of the self-made man in his widely read novels of several decades ago. As a result the multitudes who don't finish first, who never become corporate presidents or champions in their fields, are left with feelings of failure. Ironically perhaps, Alger himself is an example of the failure to live up to the American dream, as his own life was a personal disaster.

What is not mentioned in the novels or in the cultural ethics is that men with power and money tend to pass on their money and power to their children. And children of poor parents tend to produce children who grow up poor despite a desire to rise above their conditions. This is not always true, however; real social and economic opportunities do exist in this great country. We must remember that America has a comfortable middle class that includes the grandchildren and great-grandchildren of lower classes that migrated to America at the turn of the last century. Most of those who have acquired money and power, however, are white, protestant, and from northwest Europe.

A few people began to challenge the cultural illusion of social Darwinism during the Great Depression when very able and willing men were unable to find work of any sort, much less the great jobs associated with money and power. They were not the sole determiners of their destiny. Impersonal enemies, such as economic conditions, prevented people from being self-reliant.

Using popular symbols of physical strength, David in Psalm 147 illustrates how the Lord is not impressed with the autonomous myth of strength that is ingrained in the American mind. David records, "He does not delight in the strength of the horse; He takes no pleasure in the legs of a man. The Lord takes pleasure in those who fear Him, In those who hope in His mercy." (vv. 10,11). David is telling us not to depend solely upon ourselves for strength. He says, "The Lord God is my strength and my shield" (Ps. 28:7).

American men, victimized by our culture, have a difficult time leaning on another person for strength, least of all God. It goes against the grain of our culture. In discussing this, Greg Risber commented, "John Wayne, who embodied the ideal man, both on and off the screen, wouldn't say, 'I'm scared but let's attack.' He says, 'Let's kill the SOBs.'" Mr. Risber belongs to the Chicago Men's Gathering (CMG), a discussion group of men who feel they've lived for thirty or forty years in a man's world that seems obsolete, unworkable, and undesirable.

In the early 1990s in this nation of widespread prosperity, an estimated thirty-three million Americans live in poverty, eight million Americans are without jobs, and three million of our citizens are homeless.

Christians must reject our culture's benign neglect—or worse, its hostility—toward those Americans who are weak or handicapped, and ask themselves, *What do I as a Christian man owe people who are not as well off as I am?* And we must reject the unrealistic and unhealthy expectations that our culture has established for so-called real men. However, our rejection of what is wrong in our culture need not be reactive. Theologian Carl F. H.

Henry says we need to do more than sponsor a Christian subculture that competes directly with secular culture in the areas of thought and action.[1] We need to act and think in a manner that is consistent with our faith and values. We are not called to be different or to be odd or reactionary. Rather, we are called to be caring and compassionate—in a word, *civilized*.

Signs of Civilization

During the nine years that I taught anthropology classes, I often asked students to define an advanced civilization. Almost every student would mention countries or cultures which had achieved a technological superiority over their contemporaries. Like most people, the students invariably associated technological advance as an indication of higher civilization. Most often mentioned was America's ability to put Neil Armstrong on the moon in 1969. Even the Quaker president of the United States at the time, Richard Nixon, referred to the lunar landing as "the greatest event in all of world history," therefore superseding creation; the birth, death, and resurrection of Christ; the formation of democracies; or the invention of vaccines. The moon landing was a mechanical triumph of the highest order, but what of our triumphs on the spiritual and human levels?

The advance of technology has been a mixed blessing. While providing comfort and convenience, it also has worked to separate us from one another. The late Francis Schaeffer pointed out that in years gone by, in the Swiss mountains, women worked with their husbands all day in the fields and then slept with them all night. Today men spend their time with tractors. This is not to debate the importance of machinery and the advantages it yields, but only to say that specialization of labor and technology may cut down the amount of time we spend with loved ones. We continue to sacrifice friendship, fellowship, and community for material things.

Scripture does not agree with this philosophy. Paul, in 2 Corinthians 4:18, lays out the criterion for civilization and the inadequacy of material things: "We do not look at the things which are seen, but at the things which are not seen. For the things which are seen are temporary, but the things which are not seen are eternal."

The mark of civilization is not material or technological advancement. Nazi Germany in the 1930s and 1940s killed millions of people efficiently and rapidly with some of the most sophisticated technology of those decades; and yet by anyone's definition the Nazis must be viewed as uncivilized.

The mark of civilization, I told my students, is how individuals and an entire culture treat the weak, those less fortunate who lack power and influence. The weak are the defenseless—those who lack strength in body, mind, or spirit. Men are not meant to dominate these people but are to emulate the servant's heart of Jesus. In the nineteenth and early twentieth centuries, the Christian community, not the social Darwinists, worked for the removal of slavery, child labor practices, inhumane prisons, and mental institutions.

Romans 14 and 15 calls us to be active in our community. We are to be involved in helping those who have real needs which they themselves are unable to satisfy. Deuteronomy 15:7–8 reads, "If there is among you a poor man . . . you shall open your hand to him, and lend him sufficient for his need" (RSV). First Timothy 6:18 instructs us "to do good, to be rich in good deeds, and to be generous and willing to share."

Late in the nineteenth century Ferdinand Tornies, a German sociologist, contrasted and generalized two distinct kinds of societies. One is *gemeinschaft* which means commitment to community, sense of belonging, moral stability, tradition, sharing of attitudes, intimacy and extended kinship, fixed status, and shared sacred values.

In sharp contrast, *gesellschaft* loosely translates as a group created for a special purpose, like a business established to pursue self-interest. People freely join this type of society and see it as a practical way of achieving certain goals. American men correspond to this kind of group. They learn early in life that they are to concentrate on pursuing their own goals and not to be too concerned with relating to people.

And yet if given the conscious choice of either freedom and convenience or community and intimacy, it would be difficult for most of us to choose. We enjoy our privacy with the knowledge that solitude can bring loneliness. Ralph Keyes, in his book *We the Lonely People*, says that above all else we Americans value mobility, privacy, and convenience. And it is these very traits that are the source of our lack of community. Of these three, privacy is our most cherished value. But it has not always been this way. Keyes reminds us, "Privacy as an ideal, even as a concept, is relatively modern. Marshall McLuhan says it took the invention of print to tear man from his tribes and plant the dream of isolation in his brain. Historian Jacob Burchardt says that before the Renaissance, Western man was barely aware of himself as an individual. Mostly he drew identity from membership in groups—family, tribe, church, guild."[2]

Francis Schaeffer, in his important book *How Shall We Then Live?*, argued that one of our most precious values in late-twentieth-century America is the desire to be left alone. We are a private people. Alvin Toffler argued twenty years ago in *Future Shock* that we can be self-sufficient as individuals. We don't need other people as previous generations did to get through life on a day-to-day basis. The introduction of time- and labor-saving technology has reduced our dependence upon others to respond to daily problems. Television alone, of course, has done much to undermine interpersonal communication.

This slide toward a *gesellschaft* culture is received with mixed feelings. Vance Packard has written that our culture, with its obsession with mobility and privacy, has produced *A Nation of Strangers*. Commenting on the stress of moving, Suzanne Gordon, author of *Lonely in America*, says she wishes she lived in a simple Chinese village where nothing changes and you know everyone from birth to death.

Mobility in the 1990s may be slowing with the growth of two-income families and with more people refusing job transfers in part due to the instability of the real estate industry. But geographical movement remains substantial, and we remain, as a culture, devoted to privacy and autonomy.

It need not be this way. Frustration and a feeling of hopelessness present us with an important cultural dilemma. Rather than wring our hands and talk about how good it used to be, we can make changes today in our own personal lives which will directly affect those we know, and through them we can change our cultural values. Yes, our society is fluid and dynamic and capable of change. Indeed, we have witnessed in our own lifetime more change than our ancestors experienced over several generations. Some of these changes have been good, while some aspects have been destructive.

Change is possible. We see it every day of our lives. Therefore we can introduce biblical principles into our culture and expect to see positive change. Our offer of friendships, our opening up to others, can be an important solace at a time when other traditional institutions are in a state of decline. Marriage, community, and—in many cases—the church no longer provide the intimacy we all need.

To begin to confront seriously the non-biblical male values of American culture, we need first to define clearly a cross-cultural masculinity that is based on Scripture.

Biblical Christian Masculinity

We need a broader definition of what it means to be masculine in the American culture. Rather than spend our time criticizing non-biblical, macho lifestyles, we should go on the offensive by providing our family, friends, and coworkers a masculinity that conforms to biblical principles.

American people are hurting and lonely. People long for connectedness and commitment. The me-first strategy is losing appeal in the 1990s as people hunger for deeper, more sustained, committed relationships. This decade can produce the "we generation."

Social scientists such as Thorstein Veblen, C. W. Mills, and Erich Fromm have told us throughout this century that we are living in a culture that is both materialist and consumption oriented. Men possess a materialistic view of both men and women: They view women as sex objects and other men as objects to be manipulated toward their own selfish ends.

Christians must work to liberate men from destructive definitions of masculinity which prevent the development of healthy interpersonal relationships. Call this a man's liberation movement if you like. The fact is men in the United States need a change. Committed Christians can be influential in the lives of other Americans as we live a masculinity that is biblical rather than American.

To be truly masculine is to be a follower and imitator of

Jesus Christ. Christ is our great example (1 Pet. 2:21). Commenting on this fact, Dr. Gary Collins lists several Christlike characteristics which we should emulate. Christ was:

1. Dependent on God for daily guidance, frequently at prayer and thoroughly familiar with the Scriptures.
2. Intolerant of sin and a firm defender of justice.
3. Compassionate and not afraid to show his feelings.
4. Knowledgeable of events around him, concerned about the poor and needy, helpful in alleviating suffering, sensitive to others, and willing to tolerate personality differences.
5. Characterized by love, joy, peace, patience, kindness, goodness, faithfulness, gentleness, and self-control.[3]

Men who use Jesus as their example for masculinity affirm that they are able to be warm, loving, caring, open, sensitive creatures. This masculinity rejects the narrow, rigid, traditional, and often destructive manly role which demands that we be tough, aggressive, and unfeeling. Christlike masculinity puts into practice both the biblical principles of friendships from Chapter 6 and the personality traits discussed in Chapter 7.

God's ways are not our culture's ways.

For example, writing over two centuries ago and referring to the United States, Alexis de Tocqueville observed, "I know of no country, indeed, where the love of money has taken a stronger hold on the affections of men." The Yuppies or young urban professionals of the 1990s are maintaining the accuracy of that observation in American culture. Many materialistic new Calvinists are climbing a success ladder—to nowhere. In Luke 16:19–31 Jesus tells a parable about a man who, like many today, accumulated both wealth and power. In our culture we would call him a success, even though he was selfish and had no concern for the beggar Lazarus at his gate. Moreover, he paid the ultimate cost for his "success." He ended up in hell, while Lazarus, a failure on the basis of our culture's standards, went to heaven.

The application of biblical knowledge and principles can not only change your life and the lives of those around you but also can extend to the larger culture. It seems to me that we are missing a golden opportunity in this generation to really help individuals see the bankruptcy of contemporary culture. What is highly valued within our culture may well be detestable to God (Luke 16:15), but not because he doesn't want us to enjoy life. On the contrary, the Bible teaches that God wants us to live life to the fullest. To accomplish this we must live within and in accordance with certain given physical, psychological, and moral laws or principles—all given to us by God himself in the Bible.

What we perceive "through a glass darkly" to be gold, silver, and precious stones may actually be wood, hay, and stubble. To positively influence the lives of others at this time in our nation's history, we must be able to distinguish between our culture's values and Christianity's.

Vernon C. Grounds, former president of Conservative Baptist Seminary in Denver, reminds us that successful people in history like Jesus, Paul, Peter, and Stephen are usually in conflict with their culture. Our culture has little time for the criteria God has established for us in our dealings with others. God's measure of a man is Christlike love (1 Cor. 13:1–3) which produces a servant's heart and behavior (Matt. 20:25–27). But this is a far cry from the mental images of masculinity we have perpetuated in our culture.

A point of clarification needs to be made here. A servant's heart should not be equated with a milquetoast Christian acquiescence to our culture. At a meeting I heard a man say, "I'll admit I'm a Christian, but I feel that pornography is wrong." Admit? Admit what? The poor fellow was defensive and nervous as he attempted to articulate his faith while apologizing for it all in the same sentence.

I don't know which is worse, an anemic, halfhearted comment or no comment at all. Somehow I think silence is preferable to a weak-willed, half-believed defense of the biblical world view. Even though our beliefs may be in the minority, we need not be apologetic. In any event, you don't determine what is true or right by a head count. By the time the man said, "I'll admit I'm a Christian, but . . ." he had already lost the respect of his audience, both Christians and non-Christians alike. Between the extremes of weak-willed spirit and harsh arrogance lies a quiet, informed confidence that is needed.

What can you do in a practical and positive way to alter the culture you live in? I suggest you evaluate your own thinking and behaving, making sure you're part of the solution rather than part of the problem. Begin with the culture of your home, then your church, and then your community. Following are a few ideas to help you evaluate your performance in these three subcultures.

In Your Home

Traditional cultural images of masculinity have treated women as objects to be manipulated, ignored, patronized, or in other ways not taken seriously. Macho men are rarely respected by mentally well-adjusted women. For a man to cling to a macho attitude is both insensitive and immature from a biblical perspective. The Bible indicates that a man should be other-person oriented. We should love and care for our wives as we do ourselves (Eph. 5:28,33).

Peter tells husbands that they should give honor to their wives and share everything with them (1 Pet. 3:7–11). While no one knows for sure, I think Peter may have written this section of Scripture after he had an argument with his wife. Imagine the following situation: Peter comes home after a hard day of working with Jesus. Instead of asking his wife about her day, he says in a demanding way, "When do we eat?" Learning that they will have fish for dinner in a few minutes, he blurts out with, "What? Fish again?" Or perhaps she wanted to talk with him and he didn't listen. More than likely Peter, like many of us at the end of the day, took his wife and family for granted.

Following a tough day with the kids, washing the clothes at the river, and cooking the evening meal, Peter's wife wasn't prepared for his insensitivity. She may have left the room in tears. Feeling sorry for himself, Peter may have turned to God, "What's wrong with her? I don't understand her sometimes. I try to be a good husband." Peter's prayer doesn't get any higher than his family room ceiling. About this time the Holy Spirit within Peter may have given him verse 7 of 1 Peter 3, which told him, and tells us, that if a husband doesn't live with his wife in an understanding, loving way, his prayers will be virtually worthless. Prayer is never to be used as a substitute for obedience. Realizing his mistake, Peter must have taken the initiative and gone to his wife, comforting her and saying—and meaning—those two difficult words, "I'm sorry." She was gracious and accepted his apology. Only after his reconciliation with his wife was Peter able to communicate again directly with God. Perhaps to summarize the lesson he had just learned, Peter wrote in verse 8, "Finally, all of you, live in harmony with one another; be sympathetic, love as brothers, be compassionate and humble."

Our culture has taught us that historically it is a woman's responsibility to raise the kids. This mindset is slowly changing. The culture may be responding to our basic needs. As pediatrician Lee Salk claims, "Men have always had a need to be tender and to nurture." Our culture has only recently begun to acknowledge this need, possibly due to the large number of working women. The first significant discussion of the father's role in parenting surfaced following the release of movies such as *Kramer vs. Kramer*. Whatever the recent cultural shifts, the Bible has cited for thousands of years the important role fathers should occupy with their children. As is also true for women, men have the responsibility and the privilege to raise children properly and with love (Deut. 6:2,5). Macho harshness and insensitivity must be avoided (Col. 3:21). At the same time, concerned, involved discipline must be exercised (Eph. 6:4).

Of course, an American man doesn't have to be either a husband or father to exercise biblical masculinity. Dr. Gary Collins reminds us that Jesus never married and, possibly, neither did Paul, yet both were exemplary masculine personalities.

Married or not, parent or not, the biblical masculine man treats women and children the same way he treats men—with love and respect.

In the Church

I asked the members of my adult elective Sunday school class what they as individuals could do to befriend both the new and established members of our church. Their comments were interesting: "Welcome the new people with a smile and a handshake"; "Be hospitable"; "Invite

new people to your home for lunch following the service";
"The important thing is not to be pushy but to be available." All agreed that a new person's race, educational
level, or income shouldn't matter; we should treat them
all alike.

A class member said that with established church people, "We should be available in time of need, not overbearing but there if needed." Another man, a deacon,
said, "We should be sensitive to people who are lonely or
experiencing some fellowship need."

This is all fine in theory, but our churches, like other
institutions, are affected by the impersonality of our culture. Most cult experts agree that many young people turn
to cults and strange sects because they provide at least the
appearance of emotional support and love which is lacking in many of our evangelical churches.

Following their conversions to Christ, Henry and
Marion Jacobsen said that it was difficult to find in a
Bible-believing church "the total acceptance and genuine
fellowship (which) we took for granted among the
Mormons."[4]

Often our principal contact in a new church is with an
official greeter, dutifully commissioned and recognizable
by his carnation or ribbon. It is his assigned official duty
to be nice. The non-greeters sit with their own group and
rarely venture forth to meet new people. In one evangelical church a friend of mine attended for several weeks,
visitors were told to meet at a certain table for coffee and
fellowship following the service. He and his wife took up
the challenge and congregated at the visitors' table. Despite their best efforts, after several weeks this gregarious
young couple were not made to feel welcome. They left
this church and continued their search for a friendly
church family.

Our churches copy our culture's corporate model of ef-

ficient impersonality. We emphasize structure and organization which often lack spontaneity and love for one
another. Not so with the early church! Several years ago
David Mains wrote a book, *Full Circle*. He argued that
rather than try to get new people to fit into the existing
church structure, we should alter the structure to allow
people the opportunity to express in ministry the gifts
given to them by God. Pastor Mains was saying that the
church needs to be more human, more interested in
people. Larry Richards, commenting about a research
project dealing with those whom evangelicals turn to in
time of need, said that when a personal crisis strikes we're
more likely to turn to volunteer community organizations
than to a pastor or church friends.[5]

Most of us are instinctively defensive when we hear any
type of criticism of our church. But we need to realize
that the impersonality of our culture has infiltrated our
churches. We often pay lip service to Christian values,
while in reality we conform to cultural norms more than
we realize.

It need not be this way. You can be distinguishable from
those who are fully immersed in American culture. As
with other areas of your life, you'll need to make a conscious effort to change. Change in small ways at first—
smile, say hello, initiate a short conversation, ask fellow
parishioners about themselves, be an unofficial greeter.
Your greeter status will be recognized because of your inward thoughtfulness, not because of an external ribbon or
carnation.

For certain people and occasions you'll need to make a
phone call, pay a visit, or write a letter of encouragement.
Encourage small *koinonia* groups within the church
where individuals can get to know one another better in a
spiritual and social environment. Don't always sit with
the same group or in the same pew during church func-

tions, but rather reach out to others. Encourage lay-person participation in the different ministries of the local church.

Invite single persons and families to your home for fellowship. A large meal is not necessary to exercise the gift of hospitality. If someone is in need, don't say, "Call me if you need help." No one will call. Rather say, "I'll bring dinner Monday night," or "I'll drive you to the hospital," or "I'll be over Saturday morning to help in any way I can."

To be transformed in our relationships (Rom. 12:2) requires that we treat people as whole persons—holistically. From witnessing to strangers to helping a friend in need, we are required to see people as total beings—people with fears, hurts, grudges, loves, ambitions. People fill many roles other than just church attenders; they are employees, parents, marriage partners, citizens, and taxpayers, to name a few.

Like our larger culture, the churches have lapsed into a spectator society. In society we passively watch sports instead of playing ourselves. We listen to Amy Grant, Sandi Patti, or other gifted musicians instead of getting the family around the piano and singing ourselves. We listen too often to the multitudes of so-called experts instead of thinking ourselves, seeking the wisdom and counsel of friends, and using the brains God gave us.

The church, of all places, should be culturally transformed. We should be different. We should be a family of brothers and sisters who care for each other. We are told we will be known by our love for one another (John 13:34–35).

As in a modern family, members of a church family should lighten the load of fellow believers when their individual burdens become extensive (Gal. 6:2). Amish groups take this verse literally. For example, if a man loses his barn to fire or a tornado, his friends and fellow church members, without being asked, work together until a new barn is constructed. Breaks are taken during construction to eat food prepared at the work site by the wives. Due to this level of commitment to each other, Amish tend to feel that insurance, such as social security, is unnecessary. In practical ways we too are to help those in need (James 2:14–17).

Don't confuse culture and lifestyle with true Christian piety. We often become offended when someone doesn't conform or comply with our cultural brand of Christianity. My wife and I were both church youth leaders during the late 1960s and early 1970s. As you recall, this was a period of social upheaval, which included the so-called Jesus movement. Our college-age youth group sponsored many activities, socials, and home Bible studies in an effort to reach out to unchurched young people. The group successfully reached many with the gospel of Jesus Christ. Several began to attend the regular services of the church and to grow in their new faith.

One would think the church leaders would have been pleased with this outreach. However, many of these new, young Christians did not conform to accepted conservative clothing styles. And many had long hair which really irritated the board of deacons. In fact, I was called before the church and required to answer questions about why I was encouraging these "long-haired Communists" to worship in our church.

I tried to explain that they were not Communists and while I personally didn't care much for long hair on males, it seemed a minor point. We should be tolerant and accepting of others, I argued. Besides, isn't it more important what goes on inside of one's head rather than how long hair grows on the outside? Anyhow, many Christians throughout history had long hair. I even showed them a picture of the great English preacher Charles Spurgeon. He was sporting long hair and a full beard.

It was no use. The majority of the deacons had fallen prey to the notion that their brand of conservative American culture—in this case, fashion—was somehow Christian. The witness of that church suffered because it majored on what was minor or even irrelevant and had little time left over for caring, loving, and accepting those who might be different. Some of the established church members also seemed to resent that these long-haired people really tried to live as Jesus taught.

Do you need to gain victory over some kind of cultural trap that prevents you from reaching out to others? Reading good books can help. Catherine Marshall wrote in *Something More* that we must release others from our judgment. In the process we release ourselves to be free to love others whom God leads into our lives. We are admonished to put aside cultural distractions and to accept one another (Rom. 15:7) just as Christ has accepted us. Pastor Jerry Cook, in his book *Love, Acceptance and Forgiveness*, wrote from his heart how a church can truly reach out to others without letting cultural differences create adverse dissensions. Practical love, not judgment, is the way.

We need to see better what God wants of us without being hindered by viewing through a dark, cultural looking glass. *Christianity Confronts Culture* by Marvin Mayers, while written for missionaries, is useful in helping any Christian "see" his culture more objectively. Another book that exposes the secularization of American Christianity is *The Gravedigger File* by Os Guinness.

A few years ago evangelicals began to recognize that the church, like other institutions, can be adversely affected by culture. In 1982 Lloyd Perry and Norman Shawchuck wrote *Revitalizing the Twentieth-Century*

Church. These authors realize that the church has experienced interpersonal problems and cultural contamination, but with prayer and God's help, the future will be better.

In Our Community and Country

For too long, evangelicals have been uneasy with expressing their ideas in social settings other than church. This is partially because of feeling inferior or wanting to be liked, and partially because of not wishing to offend another person. But it's okay to share your ideas. Indeed it is essential. In fact it's okay to confront other ideas that are wrong from a biblical perspective. Caution: Confront the issue, not the person. Unless you can have a healthy exchange of ideas with someone, you don't experience interpersonal communication at its best. You need both honest confronting and real caring in a good relationship.

In his excellent book *Caring Enough to Confront*, David Augsburger lists how to care and confront at the same time.

Caring	Confronting
I care about our relationship.	I feel deeply about the issue at stake.
I want to hear your view.	I want to clearly express mine.
I want to respect your insights.	I want respect for mine.
I trust you to be able to handle my honest feelings.	I want you to trust me with yours.
I promise to stay with the discussion until we've reached an understanding.	I want you to keep working with me until we've reached a new understanding.

Caring	Confronting
I will not trick, pressure, manipulate, or distort the differences.	I want your unpressured, clear, honest view of our differences.
I give you my loving, honest respect.	I want your caring-confronting response.[6]

Dr. Augsburger is right on the mark. I have a distant relative who is a Christian. This person refuses to discuss any and every topic on which we might possibly hold differing views; this is meant to keep our relationship pleasant and pleasing to God. But the fact is we really don't have a relationship. We exchange trivial comments, pass on plastic smiles, and that's it. How much better to both care and share as Augsburger suggests.

Robert Louis Stevenson once said to travel hopefully is better than to arrive. We must realize that our world is not and will not be perfect until Christ returns to this planet. Stan Mooneyham, former president of World Vision, recalled that John Bunyan did not title his book *Pilgrim's Destination* but rather *Pilgrim's Progress*. We have not arrived. We should not be discouraged but rather should work to improve the lives of individuals and the social institutions that so greatly influence all of us.

We must have hope if we are to influence our culture and nation. Don't give up on America or its people. Too many evangelicals have given up mentally, deciding to sit in a mental rocking chair and wait for the Second Coming. The parable of the savorless salt may apply to many of us today (Matt. 5:13).

Our nation is suffering from a decline in absolute biblical values similar to the period of Jewish history when "every man did that which was right in his own eyes" (Judg. 21:25 KJV). The result for America has been moral decline, injustice, and flashes of political chaos.

A few years ago when CBS television was being criticized for the sex and violence presented in its programs, CBS vice president at the time, Arnold Becker, made a revealing (and to me shocking) statement: "I'm not interested in culture. I'm not interested in promoting social values. I have only one interest—that's whether people watch the program. That's my definition of good; that's my definition of bad."

Without a moral foundation a nation usually degenerates into a state of anarchy. Humans cannot long endure chaos where everyone does his own thing. The absence of a national structure of absolute values ultimately leads to revolution and dictatorship. This pattern has been repeated over and over in world history.

Writing several decades ago, theologian J. Gresham Machen said you can remove the engineer from a train and witness little initial impact. The train may coast for several miles before stopping. In America, with a crisis of leadership and morality, we may coast for several years. Eventually, however, a day of reckoning will occur.

If *Time* magazine is correct, some 40 million people in America claim to be born again. This should have a significant impact on our culture. To truly influence the culture for good takes a positive noncomformist. Yes, a nonconformist. *The Living Bible* paraphrases Romans 12:2 as follows: "Don't copy the behavior and customs of this world, but be a new and different person with a fresh newness in all you do and think." We can influence our culture, especially in a free society based upon a democratic form of government.

The writer in 2 Chronicles 7:14 recorded the Lord's conditions for cultural and spiritual change: "If my people, who are called by my name, will humble themselves and pray and seek my face and turn from their wicked ways, then I will hear from heaven and will forgive their sin and will heal their land."

Some Christians are beginning to realize that one person's influence can impact the social world of the late twentieth century. Indeed we are witnessing a return of fundamentalists to an active involvement in public life. I believe *Listen America,* authored by Jerry Falwell, is the manifesto for this movement. For decades, other more liberal Christians such as Dr. David Moberg in *The Great Reversal: Evangelism Versus Social Concern* and Senator Mark Hatfield in *Conflict and Conscience* have argued for evangelical participation in public life for the purpose of changing individual lives as well as social institutions. Another voice for this position was that of Francis Schaeffer, in books such as *How Shall We Then Live?* and *Whatever Happened to the Human Race?*

Evangelicals hold different views on the issues that confront us and how to solve our nagging and perplexing social problems. But our oneness in Christ, our dependence on Scripture, prayer, and the direction of the Holy Spirit unite us, make us one in Christ as we individually and collectively influence this great nation.

We may as evangelicals disagree on issues such as the defense policy, capitalism, welfare, and secular humanism, but we can all agree to be caring, concerned, biblically masculine men who reach out to people in need. The lesson of the Samaritan is that we are not taking time from our lives when we befriend others; we are living our lives to the fullest.

DISCUSSION QUESTIONS

1. Moses rejected Egypt's lifestyle. What aspects of America's culture should we reject?
2. If *Time* magazine is correct that there are approximately 40 million born-again Americans, why are evangelicals not having more of an impact on the American culture?

3. How do Christ's masculine traits as listed by Dr. Collins differ from your own? What ideas do you have to help you conform to Christ's example?
4. List some positive ways we can change our culture by exerting a biblical masculinity.
5. How can we distinguish cultural beliefs from Christian faith? When you apply that criterion to *your* beliefs, which ones are cultural and which are really Christian?

CHAPTER THIRTEEN

How Can a Woman Help?

At the still point of the turning world.
—T. S. Eliot

The message of this chapter is mainly for your wife, or perhaps your sister, girlfriend, or mother. I suggest that you share this chapter with the important woman in your life and solicit her support as you work to enhance the quality of your relationships with other men. Now on to the chapter.

Women *Can* Help

Admittedly men are not always easy to understand. And they are even more difficult to relate to. In recent years there have been several best-selling books that attempt to define the problems that beset men in relationships and provide suggestions on how to both understand and relate to men better. A few of the books are *Smart Women, Foolish Choices* (Sonya Rhodes and Marilyn Potash), *Men Who Hate Women and the Women Who Love Them* (Susan Forward **187** and Joan Torres), *How to Love a Difficult Man* (Nancy Good), *The Samson and Delilah Complex* (Eva Magolies and Louis Genevie), *Men Who Can't Love* (Steven Carter and Julie Sokol), *Women Men Love, Women Men Leave* (Connell Cowan and Melvyn Kinder), *The Peter Pan Syndrome: Men Who Have Never Grown Up* (Dan DeKiley), and *Cold Feet: Why Men Won't Commit* (Sonya Rhodes and Marilyn Potash).

A common thread throughout these books is that men are not very well adjusted, they are unwilling to form committed relationships with women or other men, and women themselves are not to blame for the interpersonal relationship problems confronting men.

Then you may have read the magazine articles and books that offer advice on how to keep the man in your life happy—massage his ego, say only what he wants to hear, pretend to be what he wants you to be, indulge his every whim. In seminars and books exemplified by Marabel Morgan's *The Total Woman* in the seventies, women are told to submit to the president of the family—the man. You are told to revere and even worship him by following the four A's: accept, admire, adapt, and appreciate.

These conservative generalizations and oversimplifications sound good and, indeed, contain a measure of truth, but they often break down in the real world of complex problems. When a woman is unable, despite her efforts and good intentions, to measure up to the superwoman syndrome, guilt and anger often set in. She needs a more balanced approach than that described above in order to understand and help the important man in her life.

Counselors are quick to say that a marriage partner cannot meet all one's needs. A marriage is more healthy when both spouses lead integrated lives. In cases where you find a man who says, "My wife is the only true friend

I can turn to," you will also find a wife who says, "I only wish he'd find a friend." A wife cannot meet all the emotional needs of her husband, nor can he meet all of hers.

As a man I tend to want to reject this idea. I want to think I can meet all the needs my wife might have. Grudgingly, however, I must admit that I cannot be all things to even one person. While I believe strongly that husband and wife should be the closest of friends and the marriage relationship is far more important than a friendship, there is room and need for same-sex friendships.

Just in case of any misunderstanding, I want to emphasize that friendships outside marriage, while important, must not interfere with family activities. A husband and wife's principal responsibility in human relationships is to each other and to their children. You must protect your family's time together and not allow a friendship to steal inordinate amounts of time from the family. Close friendships established on the biblical model realize the importance of the marriage and family relationships, and therefore do not allow the friendship to compete with family responsibilities.

When I was a guest on James Dobson's "Focus on the Family" program, I was asked if my emphasis on the importance of male friendships might negatively affect family life. My answer was "No." Friendship should complement marriage and family life, not compete with it for attention. Friendships, like community and church service, make a man a better father and husband as long as the principal focus of his life remains his family. The fact remains, however, that men need friends, and if those relationships are biblical, they will enhance rather than detract from the marriage relationship. Husbands need quality friendships to add balance and sharing to their way of living.

How can you help the man in your life develop close

interpersonal relationships? I asked women to respond to this in questionnaires. Their answers include the following:

"Encourage him to see his friends in our home; allow him time."

"Encourage him to reach out, to be more personal, to do things with other men."

"Create an atmosphere in which he is free to grow as a person."

"Let him know it's not a crime to let his feelings show."

"I need to point out his good qualities. I need to draw him out more, to get him to express his feelings."

Almost without exception these women believe it is important to encourage their men to develop male relationships. And *encourage* is the theme of this chapter, for active encouragement is the way you will best help your husband with his interpersonal friendships.

In earlier chapters we discussed how the rigidity of the macho male prevents growth of close friendships of any quality. Psychotherapist Edward B. Fish is of the opinion that macho men would disappear like snowballs in July if women stopped making it so heavenly for them. Therefore, to help a man help himself may mean going against the grain to some extent. You may need to expand, move away from the traditional and narrow definition of a woman's role.

You can help your husband set priorities for his activities and thinking that coincide with biblical values. Jerry and Mary White in their book *The Christian in Mid-Life* report that all too often a man awakens too late and discovers that his family and friends have lived for years in the shadow of his work and ambition. A wife should encourage her husband to lead a more enjoyable, balanced life which includes—in moderation—each of the following: work, play, church, community service, family, and friends.

Establish a Balance

Norman Wright believes that:

The more a man centers his identity in just one phase of his life—such as vocation, family, or career—the more vulnerable he is to threats against his identity and the more prone he is to experience a personal crisis. A man who has limited sources of identity is potentially the most fragile. Men need to broaden their basis for identity. They need to see themselves in several roles rather than *just* a teacher, *just* a salesman, *just* a handsome, strong male, *just* a husband.[1]

Help your husband to recognize and experience his different selves. If your husband tends to become overly intellectual during discussions you may want to ask how he *feels* about the topic at hand. Give him the freedom to express his inner feelings. Make sure you don't reject his feelings once you begin to hear them, however. It's okay to be silly and moonstruck—listening together to an "oldie but goodie" tune—and then a moment later, seeing life passing by, to launch into an intellectual or spiritual discussion about life's meaning. Different moods and emotions complement our lives.

Encourage your husband to be a well-rounded human being. Too many people have a "me first" mindset. Many sad people are too concerned with themselves or their jobs rather than with their families and friends. Some men and women talk about an identity crisis—"I don't know who I am." They fail to grasp the biblical principle that identity comes not from focus on self but from concern for and relationships with other people.

It's currently fashionable to ignore relationships that require commitment—such as to parents, marriage partners, children, and friends—until we are free to be ourselves (whatever that means) no matter the cost. The end of such selfishness is usually frustration and sadness. This inordinate concern with self is unheard of in most other cultures, where family, friends, and even the community come before the individual.

Christian women need to build the confidence of their husbands and to encourage their development as well-rounded human beings. To do this requires that their husbands commit themselves to another, which is a form of self-denial. This, of course, cuts both ways, but men especially need the mature love and devotion only their wives can give. I'm convinced that there is nothing more important to a man than to know that his wife truly cares for him. And conversely, a man is quickly devastated by a wife's insensitive criticism. We as men are a vulnerable breed.

In my own life I firmly believe that my gregarious nature is largely the result of the rich, supportive relationship I enjoy with my wife, Sue Ann. Without her love and genuine concern for my welfare, I'm sure I'd be a very different person. Maybe it's the little boy that remains in all men—we need the constant support of the women we love. Sue Ann not only tells me she loves me, she gives specific reasons for her love. This is one of the greatest things a wife can do for her husband.

While I was conducting research for this book, one forty-five-year-old man I interviewed told me, "I work with men under stressful situations. These guys don't know how to express emotions. My wife has taught me to bring my feelings out. I'm a better man today because of her. She really cares about me."

Frankly, I found it difficult to write this book. Writing about intimacy, I felt somewhat obligated to share things about myself that I am not used to sharing with others. But as a result, I had some excellent discussions with my wife during the development of this book on a wide range of issues. Without this support on the home front, a man is less likely to be outgoing and concerned about others. Support at home helps a man develop his identity to his full potential.

Don't Expect Too Much

Many men, despite the accumulation of chronological adult status, remain little boys at heart. Dr. Theodore I. Rubin, monthly columnist for *Ladies Home Journal*, has said on several occasions that American society tends to produce mature women, but for some reason most men remain little boys with traits such as abnormal insesecurity, frustration, jealousy, insensitivity, and apprehension. Dr. Rubin believes women need to know that many men:

- Retain more of the "little boy" than women do the "little girl"
- Don't like to admit they are dependent
- Are fearful, jealous, and contemptuous of women
- Will not admit to soft, warm feelings that they consider feminine
- Feel they must be strong—that is, stubborn, competitive, and the like
- Are unable to establish mature man-to-man friendships because of a fear of homosexuality
- Have difficulty relating to children because of their own childlike characteristics—they see their own children as competitors for their wife's affection, time, and energy

- Are unable to measure up to masculine ideals and are prone to self-depreciation
- Won't admit that they crave affection; men want to be coddled and fussed over, especially in stressful times
- Are vulnerable to vanity and concerned with looking young and sexually appealing
- Measure self-esteem in terms of power and money
- Fear loneliness even more than women; many men are afraid of leisure time and vacations and do not adjust well to retirement since most of their psychological support is derived from work
- Are frightened by the possibility of rejection by women[2]

Men are different to be sure, and perhaps a little strange too. More than women, they are unpredictable, illogical, and often downright crazy. I hope you'll allow your husband a little madness in harmless areas. Don't require an explanation for everything. He won't always be able to provide one for all of his behavior.

Work at seeing his world through his eyes. Dr. Theodore Rubin observes that women tend to idealize men. Idealization does not leave room for human limitations, and when the man turns out to have faults or is unwilling or unable to fit the image, disappointment follows. So be realistic. In your effort to help him help himself, don't expect miracles. Human behavior is difficult to change. This is true for either positive or negative behavior. So don't expect too much.

Do we expect too much of men? Psychologist Herb Goldberg says that society has placed confusing expectations on the married male, demanding that he be all things to all people: the capable provider, the aggressive competitor, the wise father, the sensitive and gentle lover, the fearless protector, the controlled one under pressure, and the emotionally expressive person at home.

Do you add to your husband's pressure or do you ease his burdens? Are you satisfied with what he provides, or do you leave the impression that you need a larger home and he is always one raise behind?

Men change slowly in their relationships if they change at all. Billy Graham says he is amazed by men who spend days successfully analyzing a problem in their business and yet seem unwilling or incapable of analyzing what is wrong with either their marriage or friendships.

It's easy to criticize men for their general lack of nurturing relationships. To be helpful, however, a woman needs to minimize his weaknesses and build on his strengths. Be tolerant and understanding if his friendship skills evolve slowly. Remember, other men have trouble with this too, adding to your husband's difficulty. Remember also that your husband spends his days with men he must compete with or who are of either a higher or lower status. In spite of the fact that many women must also compete with coworkers, they are able to establish satisfying relationships and even friendships with their co-workers. But men have not found the workplace to be a good environment for developing friendships.

Donna, a woman about forty, told me that criticism is deadly to a marriage relationship, especially if it's done in the presence of relatives, neighbors, or friends, or as gossip behind the husband's back. She had learned over the course of her marriage that criticism is deadly to the male ego. Donna said, "I'm the one who creates the emotional tone of our home. I respect his friends and try to take at least some interest in them."

Women usually do take the initiative, and they usually reap the benefits of being concerned about others as well. I worked once as an adult education director. The best teacher to work in that program was a woman named Elizabeth Jacobson. She was not only an excellent teacher, but she truly cared about and was available for her adult students.

A few summers ago Elizabeth's fourteen-year-old daughter Karen was injured severely in a motorcycle accident. At the time Elizabeth said, "I cannot hide my emotions. I spent most of the past few weeks in tears, but I didn't cry alone. There always seemed to be someone there for me. I felt neither alone or afraid." Elizabeth was grateful for her friends and loved ones in this time of need. But there was another source of comfort in the strangers who were also confronting crisis. Elizabeth remembers the outreach of others.

> There were offers to help from parents whose children had been similarly hurt. Some called, some wrote, some simply came to me to say, "Aren't you Elizabeth? I also have a child who. . . ."
> On one particularly upsetting visit to the hospital, a woman I had never met approached me and asked, "Are you Karen's mother?" When I nodded, she said she had something to give to me—and she wrapped me in her arms.

This woman's son had lost his leg and was lying in a hospital bed with brain injuries from a motorcycle accident. She had also lost another son three years earlier in another accident. And still this woman, whose loss was greater than Elizabeth's, wanted to comfort her.

Women who reach out, who make the effort first to talk and care are not doormats for the men in their lives. The opposite is true. Women who care and share with strangers, friends, and family alike enrich their own lives and the lives of others who know them. This is the way all of us should live—men included!

In 1937, Dale Carnegie wrote a book that sold eight million copies because his advice was so practical. Some may argue that his *How to Win Friends and Influence People* is dated or even corny, but I disagree. His ideas are useful and for the most part, founded on biblical principles.

Dale Carnegie gives several principles for building friendships. The following ideas are adapted from Carnegie's book. If you apply these basic ideas in your marriage relationship, your husband will be more able to cultivate man-to-man friendships. According to Carnegie the best way to make more and lasting friendships is to get your mind off yourself and to take a genuine interest in other people. Be generous and sincere with praise when you see positive changes. Don't be critical of another's behavior. It only makes him defensive. Rather, get him to express his ideas. Listen to his ideas and be respectful of them even if you don't fully agree with what's being said.[3]

Good advice for everyone, men and women alike. We need to value and give our attention to the development of the internal things of the heart and spirit. The point of 1 Peter 3:1–6, for example, is that jewelry, clothes, cosmetics, and other externals are not very important despite what we hear daily from newspaper, radio, and TV ads. A primary emphasis on these external things will do little either to build a good marriage or help your husband form quality friendships.

Be a Positive Role Model

Before you can help a man develop friendships, your own relationship with him must be good. You must be a trusted confidante, one he feels free to turn to in time of need. And even then don't expect him to change directly because of your advice, no matter how good you know it to be. Your influence upon others results only indirectly, so if you want someone else to change, look first at your own behavior.

Talk is cheap. People can be won over without a word due to one's manner of life. In fact, a man can hardly be changed in any other fashion.

Women can be assertive in a thoughtful and gentle way which may lead a husband to a changed life. This occurred dramatically in my own life. Typically, I followed the crowd during my teen years. I had no real plans or goals of my own. Frequently I found myself in trouble in school, causing my mother grief. My father had died when I was twelve.

After three semesters of college I found little that interested me, so I dropped out. My lifestyle didn't bother me, but I had very little purpose in my life. It never occurred to me that I might be missing out on something—until I met Sue Ann Snyder in 1963. It didn't take long for me to see that she had something different. I was particularly impressed with her family. I saw an assurance, a quiet confident spirit, in Sue Ann's life. She really seemed to have everything together.

One afternoon, she told me what made her life special. She said being a Christian was a matter of faith. I couldn't do enough good works to earn my way to God. No one could. But Jesus Christ had already taken the punishment for my sins. I needed to put my trust in him. Somehow everything she told me made sense.

Our discussion was purely intellectual, but it influenced me. Later when I was alone I realized I needed God in my life. I prayed and asked God to forgive my sins, and by his grace to make me a caring person. My life was changed. God gave me contentment in place of restlessness. He gave me purpose in place of aimlessness. He exchanged my apathy for a thirst for knowledge. In the words of C. S. Lewis, "I was surprised by joy." God really did change me.

Several months later Sue Ann and I were married. Why did I respond to her sharing with me from Scripture and from her life? It wasn't her words; it was the way she lived her life. The way she lived led me to want to hear her words.

In the musical *My Fair Lady*, the character Henry Higgins asks, "Why can't a woman be more like a man?" This is one of my favorite musicals, but I think the question would be more appropriate if reversed: Why can't a man be more like a woman? From the surveys I conducted, women seem more prepared to make and keep friends. At a very personal level, this has also been my privileged experience these past twenty-five years of marriage with my wife.

Major on the Majors

Don't be distracted. Stay on track.

Perhaps you recall the time when Christ, on his journey to Jerusalem, stopped at the home of Martha and Mary. The Lord needed human fellowship as he contemplated the agony of his anticipated suffering and death.

Mary listened to Jesus as he spoke. But "Martha was distracted by all the preparations that had to be made." And Martha apparently resented her sister's seeming idleness. Martha said, "Lord, You do not care that my sister has left me to serve alone?" Jesus responded directly, "Mary has chosen that good part" (Luke 10:38–42).

Martha's concern with the meal is not wrong in itself. We all have to eat. Both sisters loved Jesus and were doing what they thought best at the moment. But timing and priorities must be considered. D. L. Moody's observation was that the good is often the enemy of the best. This was true for Martha during the Lord's visit. You must guard against and be aware of the barren busy life. Women are particularly susceptible to this danger because of the endless tasks that must be accomplished on the domestic front. Set lesser matters aside frequently and concentrate upon developing and nurturing an in-depth relationship with your husband. Don't neglect that which you know to be important.

Read together. Share ideas together. Listen to each other. Take a long drive and talk about anything and everything. Schedule a break in the routine. Have breakfast together. Walk or exercise together. Plan to spend some time together each day *without distractions.*

Plan for the Future

Kids make friends easily. When my family moved into a different community in 1989, my eleven-year-old son Cameron had made friends with several of the neighborhood children even before our furniture and belongings were off the moving van. Children seek personal bonds because of a need for love. Only later do they learn to suppress these needs. Parents teach their kids, especially boys, to stop being so outgoing. So in addition to helping your husband, you can begin to impact the next generation. "The hand that rocks the cradle is the hand that rules the world." The way you rear a son now will directly influence his adult life.

This is true in all cultures. For example, Dr. Margaret Mead, in her book *Sex and Temperament in Three Primitive Societies,* pointed out that a strong association exists between child-rearing practices and later personality development. Children who received a good deal of attention and gentleness, as among the New Guinea mountain Arapesh, became cooperative, unaggressive, friendly adults. But children of the New Guinea Mundugomor community, who were raised with perfunctory and intermittent attention, developed into uncooperative, aggressive, and unfriendly adults. The Bible records in Proverbs 22:6, "Train up a child in the way he should go, And when he is old he will not depart from it."

Sue Ann wrote a letter to our son when he was in second grade. He hasn't seen it yet, but perhaps when he's older she will give it to him. She had been (and still is) teaching Cameron to be affectionate and loving, even when it might be inconvenient. As her letter makes clear, Cameron got the message.

Dear Cameron:

It was a typical cold late November day today. Your friends Ken and Kristy stopped over to wait with you for a few minutes before the school bus arrived to chauffeur you to North Elementary School to Mrs. Jellison and your second grade classroom.

You announced, "Mom, the bus is coming," and out the door you and your friends went to face the world and to be the first in the bus line. Thirty seconds later you returned, rushed back into the house, up the steps, and to the window where I had been watching you. In your hurry you had forgotten to kiss me before you left. You kissed me and left again quickly, and returned to your friends.

We started most of our school days with kisses and prayers. This is the way it should be, even if you lose your place in line at the bus stop. Thanks for coming back to give me a kiss, Cameron. You made my heart smile!

Love,
Mom

What you do to and for children will have lasting influence. How do you treat your sons differently from your daughters? Do you make sweeping statements that lead your children to think of gender rather than individuals? Do you discourage your son from expressing his true feelings and emotions with a "boys don't cry" comment? Dr. Joyce Brothers suggests that you make sure your son and daughter rotate tasks such as dishes, gardening, and lawn mowing, so that these jobs are not sex oriented. Also, think before you buy toys. What impact will they have on your child? What are your kids reading at school and for leisure? Does the material reinforce distorted macho images of what is manly?

Helping Kids Make Friends is a book about teaching children to develop friendship skills. The authors advise:

- Provide many opportunities for children to interact with other kids at a very young age.
- Provide games and activities that involve children in cooperative types of play, such as painting a mural, instead of individual activities.
- Teach children to accept "no" for an answer and to realize we don't always get what we want.
- Provide plenty of models for children to learn what it means to share. For example, while watching a TV show, encourage them to notice what the good guy does to be likeable when he relates to others.
- There are lots of children's books in libraries and bookstores about friendships, making friends, moving to a new neighborhood, or losing friends. All are helpful tools as a base for talking with your child about making friends.
- If you point out other children to your child who behave well, do it in a subtle way that does not demean your youngster. For example, saying, "Look how much Sarah likes it when Johnny shares the

model airplane with her," is much more effective than, "Look how nice Johnny is; why can't you be like that?"
- We criticize our children too often. Try to notice the good things they are doing and build on that. Follow up with justified praise.
- If the parents have an easy time making friends, so will the children. Let your kids learn from your example.[4]

An important method of helping both son and father develop relationship skills is to encourage your husband to take more of the child-rearing responsibilities in your family. By spending more time with his children, a man will acquire an ability to express his emotions more fully, and the sons along with daughters will learn that it's okay for a dad to parent his children.

A dilemma faced traditionally by working women is now being confronted by increasing numbers of men in the 1990s. Frederic Hudson of Santa Barbara, California, is an example of a dad who takes parenting responsibilities more seriously. Hudson says, "I doled out my time with my children in episodic doses, then went back to the real thing—my career. All that has changed." Hudson, now fifty-five, is on his second family with two sons nine and six.

Many fathers are discovering the rewards and the responsibilities of parenting and are assuming more meaningful father roles with their kids. Dr. Samuel Osherson, author of the book *Finding Our Fathers*, writes, "Socially there is more awareness that men are not just work machines. Men have a need to nurture." Women can help their men create a balance between kids and careers and thus become better husbands, fathers, brothers, and sons. And yes, better friends!

Will *you* reach out to the man in your life?

DISCUSSION QUESTIONS

1. How can you change another person's behavior indirectly?
2. Develop a daily plan to provide the man in your life with support and encouragement. List the specifics of such a plan.
3. In what ways, like Martha in Luke 10, are you distracted from developing better communication skills?
4. Using God's promise in Proverbs 22:6, discuss the extent of our influence and responsibility as parents in helping sons develop wholesome friendships.

CHAPTER FOURTEEN

The Caring of Friendships

A man must get friends as he would get food and drink for nourishment and sustenance.
—Randolph S. Bourne

Norman Vincent Peale tells the story of a terribly upset vice president of a company who had just been passed over for the president's position. A new man had been brought in from the outside. The vice president was riled. But the new president needed the support and friendship of the vice president.

Dr. Peale advised him that tough as it might be, "I would swallow my disappointment, forget my wounded ego, walk into that man's office and tell him I wanted to help him all I could. You see, that new executive is lonely. He knows how the organization feels about him and he needs help. Believe me, he needs you. Practice empathy. Put yourself in his shoes and also try the Golden Rule on him. 'Do unto others as you wish they would do unto you.' I think it will pay off all the way around. Love 'em is the answer."

The vice president buried his pride and applied the suggestion. As a result the two men es-

205

tablished an excellent working relationship. Two years later the president moved on to a new organization. You guessed it. Before leaving he recommended that the vice president succeed him. The new president has a framed legend on the wall which reads, "Love 'Em."[1] I'm sure Dr. Peale would agree that the important thing is not that a president's position was won but rather that the two men learned to depend upon each other and developed a warm, working relationship.

Sadly this kind of relationship rarely exists in the business community where men learn early to look out for number one as they fight their way up the professional ladder.

A friend of mine who is also a superintendent of schools has discovered it is difficult to develop warm working relationships with coworkers. They are fearful, suspicious, or critical of him because of his position of responsibility. Thankfully there are a few exceptions to this, but overall he feels somewhat alone at work. To overcome such loneliness, many of us who have the position of superintendent of schools find it very useful and refreshing to meet once a month for lunch and discussion. We're becoming friends in what can be a friendless occupation.

A few years ago sociologists from Duke University interviewed hundreds of people to find out why some were happy and others unhappy. They discovered that those who are happy live in the present and future but not the past. The Duke study also found that happy people do not waste time and energy fighting conditions that cannot be changed.

Contented people, instead of complaining about not having friends, seek to enter into the lives of others. I've mentioned before, when you involve yourself in someone's life, you take risks; you're vulnerable, or at least you feel vulnerable. This risk-taking is even evident with the seemingly minor things in life such as letter writing. As the following story indicates, we must take the small risks. Take the slight chance that you'll be rejected, because to do otherwise is to miss some of the greatest joys of life.

Early in the history of our republic, the sacrifice and wisdom of John Adams and Thomas Jefferson helped to establish the new American nation. As I mentioned earlier, while they shared a love for the new United States, these two men had lost affection for each other. Some historians think that the arrogance and abrasive personality of John Adams was the cause of the falling out with Jefferson. This political and personal hostility was very noticeable when, following Jefferson's election in 1800, Adams even refused to attend the new president's inauguration.

Years passed. There was a complete lack of communication between these two statesmen. Long after Jefferson's two-term presidency, when Jefferson was sixty-eight and Adams was seventy-five, a brief letter from Adams arrived at Monticello, Virginia. Adams simply stated that he and his family were well and enclosed specimens of homespun yarn. It wasn't the content but rather the signature that gladdened the heart of Thomas Jefferson. The letter was signed, "With sincere esteem, your friend and servant—John Adams." This simple letter initiated a classic correspondence in American history.

In his excellent biography of Jefferson, Saul Padover says that "time had blunted the sharp edges of their political differences, and now that both were in retirement they could resume a friendship that was started way back when they were both comparatively young rebels against the crown."

Actually it was the concern of Dr. Benjamin Rush, also a signer of the Declaration of Independence, and an admirer of both men, who brought the two together. Of the correspondence which followed, Saul Padover says, "The two old gentlemen, both men of massive learning and vast intellectual curiosity, poured out their ideas with the zeal and zest of youngsters. To the intimacy of their letters they entrusted their innermost hopes and fears and prejudices and convictions and indignations."[2] And it must be remembered that without the concerned intervention of Dr. Rush, both Adams and Jefferson would have missed the joy that resulted from this noble relationship.

Often, however, we suffer strain in our relationships and refuse to seek reconciliation—until it's too late. The headline read "Feuding Brothers Die on Same Day." A few years ago in Dedham, Massachusetts, two brothers who had rarely spoken to each other in twenty-five years died within two hours of one another in the same emergency room. The wife of one of the brothers said that her husband was on the verge of making peace with his brother and had told her the week before that he planned to phone his elder brother. Both died of heart attacks! They never made peace over a relatively minor family dispute that took place twenty-five years earlier. How bankrupt our lives can become when we fail to reach out to others around us!

Before moving to Indiana last year, my wife and I met monthly with three other couples from our church for fellowship and Bible study. Our times together were refreshing spiritually and socially. We remember well the good conversations, laughter, and on occasion the sharing of personal concerns. A few months before we packed our bags, one of these families moved to Massachusetts. We missed them and felt a sense of personal loss.

As I was preparing to write this book, I went through all my files looking for relevant material on the subject of male relationships. In one folder I discovered a letter I had written to my friend who had gone to Massachusetts. In my letter I mentioned that we missed him and Jane and that I was looking for a new job; I wrote that Sue Ann had found a challenging women's Bible study and that the kids were doing well in school. I asked my friend David if he liked his new graduate level teaching position. I cited a few other insignificant facts and closed with "Give our love to Jane and the children." I signed the letter and then almost defensively added, "P.S. This is National Letter Writing Week. Men seem to need excuses to write."

What I have to admit is that the letter in my file is the original copy. I didn't send the letter. It's very difficult for each of us to understand our own emotions and the reasons behind our individual behavior, but I have an idea why David never received my letter.

To begin with, I didn't believe the letter was very intellectual. David is a few years older than I and very intelligent. I suspect I didn't want to seem dumb or silly to this urbane gentleman whom I respect. Also, I didn't have much to say and therefore had no reason to write. When you boil it down, one salient reason for not sending the letter emerges: I was afraid that I would be rejected. You see, I couldn't predict with accuracy how he might react to my letter, so I refused to risk possible rejection.

A few months later, when Sue Ann and I were agonizing over a possible move and change in jobs, she encouraged me to call David since he had recently struggled with a similar job change experience. I put it off. She persisted. When I finally did call, our conversation was quite enjoyable, and he gave me some ideas which helped my family deal with the new job offer. But more important, the call helped to maintain a friendship.

The lesson to be learned is this: Take the time and the risk with small things. This is how friendships begin and are maintained. Letters, smiles, luncheons, talking and listening, helping, and countless other small activities are the building blocks to friendship.

Soon after arriving in our new community and beginning a new job for a suburban Indianapolis school corporation, I received two letters from friends with whom I used to work. I was thrilled to get both letters. John's letter began: "Hope you are settled in with your family and have not started too many new curriculum projects yet." He continued, "An old Jesuit once told me to distrust any man who wants to change something before he knows what it is." I appreciated my friend John's thoughtful advice.

The other letter also produced a smile as old memories were recalled and new information shared. This letter closed with the words, "I miss you, David." I appreciated so much this man's willingness to share with me the fact that I am important to him. He lifted my spirits with his acknowledgment of our friendship and his feelings.

There is a powerful tendency to like people who like us. If the greatest truths are usually the simplest, then this is one of them. We may think that it is the romantic, exciting, and adventurous actions that attract people, but more often it is the everyday, ordinary, even mundane, acts that determine a friendship or other important relationships.

Little things really are important, aren't they? So express your friendly feelings in some small way, like writing a letter that really doesn't have to be written. (Then be sure to mail it!) Or reach out in some other way that you feel comfortable with. You'll feel better and you may reap the rich dividends of closer, more nurturing, interpersonal relationships.

Relationships are usually won or lost in the first four minutes. When we meet someone we are quick to form instant and usually lasting impressions. First impressions are not always accurate however. Major League pitcher Walt Wilhelm hit a home run at his very first time at bat. But in his long twenty-year career, he never hit another home run. While first impressions are not always accurate, they are always important.

The formula for success with new acquaintances during these critical minutes is not very complicated. We need to have direct eye contact and extend our hand as a greeting. We need to use the other person's name, ask sincere questions. And, of course, we need to smile.

Radio personality Earl Nightengale, of an earlier generation, said about meeting someone, "I'll make him glad he talked with me." Humorist Will Rogers once commented, "I never met a man I didn't like." From Dale Carnegie to Zig Ziglar, we learn that it's easy to establish positive relationships with others when we have the other person's best interest in mind. So I offer the following list of basics to you to use during the first few minutes of meeting another person.

1. Introduce yourself.
2. Offer to shake hands.
3. Smile and look at the other person.
4. Listen actively to what the other person says.
5. Remember and use the person's name.

Surely there will be people who will resist our smiles or offer of conversation. There will surely be individuals who will misunderstand our motive or will reject us and our interest in them. But these reactions should not deter us if friendship and other kinds of quality relationships do not always result from simply following some list. The point is, when our attention is other-person centered and we resist the natural fears associated with risk-taking and we establish small measurable goals, we often reap im-

provement in the quantity and quality of our relationships
with others.

You can get closer to other people and improve your
relationships by introducing small changes into your life.
Don't attempt unrealistic changes which will likely result
in failure. I would encourage you to review both the biblical principles of friendship and personality traits associated with emotional intimacy listed below and discussed
in Chapter 10. Then resolve to make daily small changes
associated with these traits.

- God centered consensus of beliefs
- Covenant
- Faithfulness
- Social involvement
- Self-disclosure
- Involvement
- Candor
- Respect
- Listening
- Acceptance
- Empathy
- Loyalty
- Compromise

For example, in reviewing the concept of involvement
you could resolve to in some way help another person each
day. This could take the form of showing your appreciation for something someone had done. Maybe it would
mean paying someone a sincere compliment or developing
more assertive listening skills. Maybe your involvement
skill could be improved by sending a letter, or making a
phone call or visiting someone in your neighborhood or at
the local nursing home. The point is to challenge yourself
to do something you're not now doing. Start today. The
dividends you'll reap will last for a lifetime.

In his book on friendship, Dr. Harold Dawley provides a summary of the rules of friendship making:

Rule 1—*Like yourself*. Think of yourself in positive ways and work toward being a friend to yourself.

Rule 2—*Reach out*. Reach out to people in subtle and direct ways so that you are in a good position for friendships to develop.

Rule 3—*Make contact*. Be accessible to people—both in the physical and psychological sense—since potential friendships surround you awaiting your contact.

Rule 4—*Be pleasant*. Strive to have a pleasing effect on people by being polite, giving genuine compliments, smiling, and engaging in similar positive behaviors.

Rule 5—*Get to know people*. Directing your interest to others and away from yourself allows you to get to know the other person.

Rule 6—*Let people know you*. Reveal personal, intimate thoughts and feelings to others at the right time, and people will be able to see and understand you as you really are.

Rule 7—*Get through to people*. Effective communication enables you to say exactly what you want so that confusion and misunderstanding are minimized.

Rule 8—*Get along with people*. Handle conflict effectively by seeing the other person's view; letting him talk it out, avoiding resentment while standing up for your legitimate rights.[3]

It's the little things like eye contact and other nonverbal signals, asking people questions, and saying thank you at the right time that make or break a relationship. Of the ten lepers healed by Christ, one—only one—wasn't suddenly too busy to return to give thanks. Dale Carnegie said, "You can make more friends in two months by becoming interested in other people than you can in two years by trying to get other people interested in you."

A group of divinity students at Princeton failed a good Samaritan test because they were in too much of a hurry. Forty unwitting theology students were asked by researchers to go across campus for a special television taping session. On their way the divinity students encountered a "victim" slumped in a doorway, coughing, groaning, and in apparent pain. Aware of a man in apparent distress, only sixteen of the forty seminarians stopped to help the man. The moral: A man in a hurry is likely to keep going and, in the process, miss opportunities for both service and friendship.

A plaque entitled "A Friend" recently caught my eye. It read, "A friend is one who knows you as you are, understands where you've been, accepts who you've become and still gently invites you to grow." Our attitude about ourselves as well as about others is important. Dr. Clyde Narramore believes that one of the important traits of emotional health is belief in your own likeableness. A second trait of emotional health is the corresponding belief that others are likeable too.

We must be aware that the people we meet in life are "okay." Don't neglect the biblical principle that all people are created and loved by God. We must, therefore, view all individuals as important and certainly worthy of our time and attention. Potential friends can be found anywhere.

Moving is always a tough job. Accumulating all that is needed (or should I say wanted?) to keep a family functioning makes moving day a mixed blessing. Our move from Northbrook, Illinois, to Noblesville, Indiana, was a case in point. Three different neighbors whom I had helped move to nearby suburbs, learning of my anticipated departure, insisted on returning the favor. So, following two high estimates from professional movers, I decided to do it myself. I accepted my previous neighbors' offer to help as well as that from some current neighbors.

The day before we moved, my wife and most—if not all—of the neighborhood women had a gigantic garage sale on our front lawn. It was a happening—buying, selling, and bartering more among each other than from the infrequent bona fide shoppers to our neighborhood flea market. We laughed and cried. Actually, the women let a few tears flow; the men, expressing their emotions a little differently, resorted to hearty handshakes.

Then on our last night in town, the Jenkins family from our church called to say good-bye. After talking briefly they said, "We're all going out for dinner." As tired as we were it would have been easier to stay at home and open a couple of cans of food. I'm glad we didn't. I'm also glad that we assented to our neighbors' offer to help.

It's easy to avoid asking or accepting help, often because we can purchase our own things and also others' services. But when we do it ourselves, we cut off the potential for discovering and developing close relationships. The result is a self-sufficient form of social isolation that leaves us lonely.

Not only did we receive help in moving, but during our search for a new home in Indiana, we were fortunate to have the help and concern of two businessmen in the city. At first I was impatient with the pleasantries and later grew skeptical of the kindness of these men. I wondered why our realtor would invite us to his home for dinner and a neighborhood cookout. When I introduced myself to a vice president of a local bank and began immediately to ask about interest rates and other related financial matters, the banker gently interrupted my inquiries with questions about my family, the move, and my new posi-

tion as curriculum director for the local school corporation. Then he said, "How do you like our town?" I finally
slowed down to listen and even share something of myself.

Finally I came to realize that these men, while businessmen to be sure, were also interested in me as a person.
Long after we purchased our home, I continued to associate with these men. The realtor and the banker may not
become lifelong close friends, but then again they may.
What's important is that they made an effort to be
friendly, and I responded. With the hustle and bustle of
house and mortgage hunting, it would have been easy to
handle everything alone, forgetting that potential friends
can be found anywhere. This illustrates the simple yet
profound truth: "To have friends, be friendly."

Expand Your Standards

Potential friends can indeed be found anywhere if
you're willing to be more aware of and open to men you
have just met as well as those you have known for years.
Even when we believe we are willing to form new friendships, usually we limit ourselves to the person who meets
our very limited criteria of a possible friend. Friends tend
to be selected from the same social class, race, political
party, and age range.

Other factors prejudice our often subconscious views
on a possible friend. My father told me shortly before his
death that a man's character may be measured by the way
he treats people who have little or no impact on his life. I
have tried to remember and practice this principle, but
not always successfully.

A poorly dressed man once asked me for a dollar so he
could get some food. I was too busy, or so I believed at the
time, to take the man to lunch. And I was unwilling to
give him the money he requested, convincing myself that

if I did give him money, he would soon turn it into a shot of whiskey or a can of beer.

But what if he really needed the money? I could have at least taken time for a little simple human conversation. All I would have lost would have been a few cents and a few minutes of my time. What I actually lost was the opportunity to involve myself in the life of another person. By keeping my money and my time, I became a loser, similar to the priest and Levite who refused to help the wounded traveler on the road outside Jerusalem. We as men need to consciously and prayerfully break out of our limited view of the world. God loves the man who asked me for money as much as he loves me. We need to pray that God will help us view the world and its inhabitants from his perspective.

It's difficult for men to take a sincere interest in others. Our thinking tends to be task oriented, not people oriented. We think of jobs to be done rather than individuals who need appreciation and recognition.

A retired milkman worked as a janitor in the high school where I taught for several years. We talked daily. Neither of us let the large difference in age and job roles prevent us from enjoying each other's company. We even asked about each other's families and personal interests.

One day as we were talking, we both realized that this dear man had known my father when they both worked for Borden Dairy. We laughed at this connection between us. He enjoyed sharing with someone who would really listen. And it was a thrill for me to discover more about my father, who had died suddenly when I was only twelve years old. It's ironic that the principle my dad taught me of extending kindness to others had helped to bring this retired man into my life.

Another older man befriended me following my father's death in 1955. Lee gave me the time and attention

I needed as an impressionable teenager. He helped me land my first real job at Hoffman Brothers Hardware in Wilmette, Illinois. It was there that Lee took the time to teach me how to work and how to live up to my potential as a worker. He even risked his life when he taught me to drive a car in a remote cemetery at age fifteen. And I'll never forget his tolerance and kindness when, misjudging the length of a pier, I wrecked the front of his boat. He knew I felt bad about what happened.

I acquired a father figure who meant a great deal to me for nearly thirty years. Before he died, I was able to return a few of his many friendly acts.

I have another friend who is several years my junior. This troubled me at first, but we share a good deal in common. We worked closely together while a church building program was under way and during these past few years have developed what I hope will be a lifelong relationship.

Don't let age differences get in your way. When you meet a man of a different age, don't immediately shut him out of your life as a potential friend.

Much of our socializing in America is done with people almost identical to ourselves. Diversity is sacrificed for humdrum similarity. Old people are isolated from the young. Rich and poor rarely meet or understand each other. The same is true for politics, religion, race, education, occupation, age, and marital status. It's as if we'll use any excuse to avoid a different kind of person.

An old people's home was constructed about a mile from the high school where I was teaching several years ago. Both buildings were off to themselves on the outskirts of town. Unlike other cultures, we in America relegate both the young and old to an unproductive, noninvolved existence. I attempted to bring these two worlds together.

Our program was called Y.O.U.—Young and Old United. It was beautiful. The two age groups learned and helped each other. In other cultures where extended families still exist, people of different ages are able to learn from and contribute to each other across the generations. Perhaps through groups like Y.O.U. or adopt-a-grandparent programs, we can reclaim an important heritage.

People of varied social or economic backgrounds rarely develop close relationships. This is somewhat understandable since diverse educational and income levels produce varied interests. The Bible warns, however, against discriminating against people of a different social class, especially the poor. From the epistle of James, for example, we learn that giving favored treatment to a man with wealth, while ignoring the poor man, is wrong (2:1–7).

Upon meeting someone for the first time, one of the first questions men ask is, "What do you do?" We want to know their social standing as well as their occupation. We hear the response to our question and then pigeonhole the person as someone to know better or someone not worth spending much time on. We get caught in the rut of equating the worth of a person with his occupation.

American values have not changed a great deal since Vance Packard wrote *The Status Seekers* in the late 1950s. The belief that what a man does for a living is the best measure of his worth is as false today as it was years ago but it's still embraced as if it were true. A man of great character may have a menial job, while someone with high status in his job may be dishonest and a failure as a parent or husband.

While researching social class differences for a sociology article, I decided to do some field work. My approach was what sociologists refer to as participant observation. For a few days I arrived at 5:30 A.M. at a day-labor employment agency on the north side of Chicago. I was poorly dressed and unshaven. At about six each day my name was called, and I was herded on a bus and driven to a factory that needed extra short-term menial help. The work was tiring. I spent all day on an assembly line packing rat poison. My pay was minimum wage.

We were like untouchables. Almost no one talked to us except to give orders. Even eye contact was rare. It was as if we didn't exist. It was an eerie feeling to be ignored. Although I was in the plant for only a few days, I had a strong desire to tell people who I really was. Since that day-labor experience, I've wondered if any of those who ignored us were middle-class Christians. Each of us wants to be recognized, even by strangers.

What I did discover is that even very poor people are willing to share. A poor man on the day-labor bus offered me conversation and half of his sandwich. Other than their poverty, and in some cases broken English, these men I worked with were indistinguishable from men of other social classes.

This is not to suggest that you should go out and search for people who are different from you. On the contrary, the best friendships are usually between people of related interests and backgrounds. The point I wish to make, however, is simply this: Relate to people as individuals, not as members of racial, economic, or social groups. Potential friends can be found in unsuspecting places—if you are willing to look.

Don't limit your friendships to popular and very likable individuals. Rather, look among ordinary people for men with great character. On an August day in 1977, Julius Loh died. Other ordinary Americans died that day, 5,478 to be exact. Some years before Mr. Loh's death, his son Jules asked his dad in irreverent jest, "Tell me, Pop, what you've done that you're proud of that no one else has done, because someday I'm going to write your obituary." Mr. Loh responded, "I've turned in three fire alarms, none false."

Writing of his father's death for the *Chicago Sun Times*, an older, wiser, sadder son recorded these words:

> In his own time, this man survived the Depression, barely, not to mention four wars and other assorted upheavals of three generations, and all the while kept both his family and his sense of humor intact.
>
> If this is an ordinary life, then genius is indeed the apt word. At least one of his children never stopped long enough in his own self-centered life to realize that fact until it was too late to realize, even that his father was mortal, that the old man would not always be there, as ordinary as a mooring post.
>
> That son, who once asked you what you were proud of, Pop, is, in his sorrow, awfully proud to bear your name.

Speaking of his dad, and for all but a handful of the others who died on that summer day, Jules Loh said, "They were born, lived decently and justly, turning in no false alarms, worked hard, honored their spouses, begat children and saw to their upbringing, minded their business and died without debt."

There are millions of good people in this world, many of whom you work with or live near. Reach out to them, really get to know them, discover their physical, emotional, and spiritual needs. The result will be warm, meaningful friendships. The love you learn to extend to others will be returned manyfold. Ask for God's help to make you a caring, concerned individual. God's love, working through you, will eliminate much of your shyness and fear.

While preparing this chapter, I asked my wife, Sue Ann, what a friendless American man should do to make and keep friends. She gave me a number of good ideas, many of which are included in this book. But one comment stood out as basic.

> Men need to view other men as individuals who have intrinsic worth and dignity as creatures of God. And therefore each person you meet is worth knowing at a personal level.

I asked Sue Ann what is the best way for men to follow through on this truth. She said, "First, a man must look for a need so he can offer help." The apostle Paul commented on this in 1 Corinthians 9:19: "Though I am free and belong to no man, I make myself a slave to everyone." "Second," Sue continued, "a man must be willing to have some of his own needs met by others."

We must stop trying to do everything by ourselves. And, at the same time, we must be sensitive to the needs of others. We will have a happier, more meaningful life if we do. Friendship, like so many good things in life, comes to those who live for others.

DISCUSSION QUESTIONS

1. Do you have one or two close Christian friends to whom you are committed by mutual agreement? If you must answer "no," would you be willing to ask God to give to you at least one such friend?
2. When you first meet another man, by what criteria do you determine whether he could be a potential friend? Discuss what occurs in the crucial first four minutes of

a new relationship. What makes these four minutes so important?

3. Do you agree that extraordinary friendships can be developed with very ordinary people? What are some benefits?

4. What do you imagine Will Rogers meant when he said, "I never met a man I didn't like"?

5. Discuss ideas for developing new friendships that were not mentioned in this chapter. Then decide how you are going to implement some of those ideas in the next few weeks.

NOTES

Chapter Two   The Best Property of All

1. Haggai 1:3–11.
2. James Wagenvoord, ed., *Men: A Book for Women* (New York: Avon, 1978), p. 165.

Chapter Three   The High Cost of Being Male

1. Dan Benson, *The Total Man* (Wheaton: Tyndale House, 1977), p. 15.
2. Roger Stamp, source unknown.
3. George F. Will, "How Reagan Changed America," *Newsweek* (January 9, 1989), p. 13.
4. "A Kinder, Gentler Job," *U.S. News and World Report* (February 13, 1989), p. 74.
5. Benson, *The Total Man*, p. 15.
6. Wagenvoord, *Men: A Book for Women*, p. 166.
7. *U.S. News and World Report* (May 10, 1976).

Chapter Four   Basic Survival Needs

1. "The Road Back," *Newsweek* (May 19, 1986), p. 26.
2. James S. House.
3. Harold Kushner, *When All You've Ever Wanted Isn't Enough* (New York: Schocken Books, 1987), p. 18.
4. Victor Frankl, *Man's Search for Meaning* (New York: Simon and Schuster, 1984).
5. Kushner, *When All You've Ever Wanted Isn't Enough*, p. 92.

224

6. John Powell, *The Secret of Staying in Love* (Niles, IL: Argus Communications, 1974).
7. Larry Crabb, *Inside Out* (Colorado Springs: NavPress, 1988), pp. 166, 165.

Chapter Five   What's the Difference?

1. Margaret Mead, *Sex and Temperament in Three Primitive Societies* (New York: William Morrow and Co., Inc., 1963).
2. "Men vs. Women," *U.S. News and World Report* (August 8, 1988), p. 54.
3. *USA Today*, February 10, 1989, p. 1.
4. Sydney J. Harris, *The Best of Sydney J. Harris* (Boston: Houghton Mifflin Co., 1976), pp. 101–102.

Chapter Six   Biblical Principles of Friendship

1. Jerry Jenkins, "Best Friends," *Moody Monthly* (August, 1989), p. 6.

Chapter Seven   Friendship Qualities We Look for in Others

1. Lee Iacocca, *Iacocca: An Autobiography* (Boston: G. J. Hall, 1985), p. 138.

Chapter Eight   The Stages of Friendship

1. Herb Goldberg, *The Hazards of Being Male: Surviving the Myth of Masculine Privilege* (New York: New American Library, 1977), p. 136.
2. Daniel Levinson *et al.*, *The Seasons of a Man's Life* (New York: Alfred A. Knopf, 1978), p. 335.
3. Joseph Bensman and Robert Zilienfeld, "Friendship and Alienation," *Psychology Today* (October, 1979), p. 59.
4. Thomas F. Powers, *Introduction to Management in the Hospital Industry* (New York: John Wiley and Sons, Inc., 1979).
5. Mary B. Parless, "The Friendship Bond," *Psychology Today* (October, 1979), p. 50.
6. Maxine Hancock, *The Forever Principle* (Old Tappan, NJ: Fleming H. Revell Co., 1980), p. 78.

Chapter Nine   Friendship in Other Times and Places

1. Robert Bell, *Worlds of Friendship* (Beverly Hills, CA: Sage Publications, 1981), p. 99.
2. George Santayana, in Robert R. Bell's *Worlds of Friendship*, p. 96.
3. Merrill C. Tenney, ed., *Zondervan's Pictorial Bible Dictionary* (Chicago: Zondervan, 1969), p. 898.

Chapter Ten   Understanding Yourself

1. Peter Johnson, "It's a Slow Healing," *USA Weekend* (December 10, 1989), p. 5.
2. Ann Landers/Creators Syndicate, "Dear Ann Landers," *Indianapolis Star*, May 30, 1986, p. 32. Used by permission.
3. Leo Buscaglia, *Living, Loving and Learning* (New York: Holt Rinehart Winston, 1982), p. 201.
4. C. S. Lewis, *The Four Loves* (New York: Harcourt, Brace, and World, 1960).

Chapter Eleven   Setting Goals for Change

1. Norman Vincent Peale, "Loving One Another Is a Sure Fire Way to Have a Merry Christmas," *Indianapolis Star* (December 20, 1986), p. 17.
2. Kathleen Catrett, "Reconciliation Costs," *Decision*, (June, 1986), p. 34.
3. O. Quentin Hyder, *The Christian's Handbook of Psychiatry* (Old Tappan, NJ: Fleming H. Revell Co., 1977), p. 144.
4. A book that examines the problems and suppositions of psychology is *Psychology As Religion: The Cult of Self-Worship* by Paul Vitz (Grand Rapids: William B. Eerdmans, 1977).

Chapter Twelve   Confronting American Culture

1. Carl F. H. Henry, *Twilight of a Great Civilization* (Wheaton, IL: Crossway Books, 1989).
2. Ralph W. Keyes, "We the Lonely People," *Intellectual Digest* (December, 1973), p. 26.
3. Gary Collins, "Search of Christian Macho," *Moody Monthly* (July-August, 1976), pp. 53–56.

4. Henry and Marion Jacobson, "The Sin Most Churches Deny," *Moody Monthly* (January, 1981).
5. Larry Richards, "The Great American Congregation: The Illusive Ideal?", *Christianity Today* (November 21, 1980), p. 23.
6. David Augsburger, *Caring Enough to Confront* (Ventura, CA: Regal Books, 1980), p. 15.

Chapter Thirteen   How Can a Woman Help?

1. H. Norman Wright, *Seasons of a Marriage* (Ventura, CA: Regal Books, 1982), p. 75.
2. Theodore I. Rubin, "What Women Don't Understand About Men," *Ladies Home Journal* (September, 1973), p. 24.
3. Dale Carnegie, *How to Win Friends and Influence People* (New York: Simon and Schuster, 1982).
4. S. Holly Stocking, Diane Arezzo, and Shelly Leavitt, *Helping Kids Make Friends* (Allen, TX: Argus Communications, 1981).

Chapter Fourteen   The Caring of Friendships

1. Norman Vincent Peale, reprinted in the *Indianapolis Star* (1981), via Ann Ackers' featured syndicated column.
2. Saul K. Padover, *Jefferson: A Great American Life and Ideas* (New York: Mentor Books, 1970), pp. 163, 164.
3. Harold H. Dawley, *Friendship: How to Make and Keep Friends* (Englewood Cliffs, NJ: Prentice-Hall, 1980), pp. 118, 119.